INSIDE ARCHITECTURE

Graham Foundation / MIT Press Series in Contemporary Architectural
Discourse

*Achtung Architektur! Image and Phantasm in Contemporary Austrian
Architecture*
Eeva-Liisa Pelkonen

Inside Architecture
Vittorio Gregotti

——————————— INSIDE ARCHITECTURE ———————————

Vittorio Gregotti

Translated by Peter Wong and Francesca Zaccheo

Graham Foundation for Advanced Studies in the Fine Arts
Chicago, Illinois

The MIT Press
Cambridge, Massachusetts
London, England

Publication of this book has been supported by a grant from the Graham Foundation for Advanced Studies in the Fine Arts.

This book was set in Melior by The MIT Press and was printed and bound in the United States of America.

Library of Congress Cataloging-in-Publication Data

Gregotti, Vittorio.
   [Dentro l'architettura. English]
   Inside architecture / Vittorio Gregotti ; translated by Peter Wong and Francesca Zaccheo.
     p.   cm.
   Includes bibliographical references.
   ISBN 0-262-57115-3 (pb : alk. paper)
    1. Architecture—Philosophy.   I. Title.
NA2500.G67913   1996
720'.1—dc20   96-15523
                                 CIP

CONTENTS

Of the many critics and theorists who enter the lists of architectural thought today, not one has been of such enduring importance as Vittorio Gregotti, not least for his exceptional clarity and longevity; in the first instance as an editor, scholar, and teacher and in the second, but of no less consequence, as an architect who has been in practice for nearly forty years. It is this combination of theory and practice that has bestowed upon his discourse such subtlety and conviction, since all of his writing has arisen out of a dichotomous process in which the critical subject constantly oscillates between the textual and the tectonic, that is to say, between the daily act of reading and writing and the equally creative struggle broached each day with his professional colleagues and collaborators.

Like other Italian architects of his generation, Gregotti found his feet as an intellectual as one of the young Turks that served under the leadership of Ernesto Rogers on the editorial staff of *Casabella,* during its second incarnation from 1949 to 1958. In the company of Aldo Rossi, Giorgio Grassi, and Guido Cannella, Gregotti participated in Rogers's rereading of the history of the early modern movement in order to integrate its legacy into postwar European practice. Thus, in issue after issue, the work of Adolf Loos, Peter Behrens, H. P. Berlage, and Hans Poelzig came to be photogenically presented and analyzed for what their finest achievements could still bestow upon the evolution and enrichment of twentieth-century architectural form. Gregotti would continue with a similar genre of research during his editing of *Edilizia Moderna,* which did much to restore the reputation of the anti-futurist Novecento movement as this had manifested itself in Italy from around 1914 to the mid-twenties; from say Giorgio De Chirico's *Nostalgia for the Infinite* of 1914 to Giovanni Muzio's Ca' Brutta apartments, completed in Milan in 1923. No one could then have imagined that the metaphysical, atectonic syntax of the Novecento that had served as the *parti pris* for the prewar Italian rationalist movement would also do the same for the Italian neo-rationalist movement of the mid-sixties, the so-called Tendenza, turning in part upon the revival of the typological method in the writings of Giulio Carlo Argan.

Unlike the leading architects of the Tendenza that became recognizable as a significant position in the Milan Triennale of 1966, Gregotti resisted the reductivist aspects of this reinterpretation of earlier Italian rationalism that was latent in the initial projects of Rossi and Grassi. Unlike the "degree zero" approach adopted by these architects, along with their typo-morphological implications, Gregotti kept his faith with the structural rationalist tradition as this had been evident in postwar Italy in the work of such architects as Carlo Scarpa, Franco Albini, Gino Valle, and even in that of Rogers himself, particularly in his Torre Velasca erected in Milan in 1958. As a result there was something almost Perretesque about Gregotti's early work in Novara, where the *modénature* derived from the mode of construction; that is to say, from a syncopated expression that articulated only too precisely the interaction between the structural frame, the brick skin, and the precast concrete window surrounds, together with other accoutrements executed in the same material.

A comparable articulation but at a mega-scale would appear almost thirty years later in Gregotti's University of Calabria of 1986, where a typo-morpho, tectonic assembly would be developed as a territorial intervention. This "viaduct block" was a didactic demonstration of Gregotti's critical/creative strategy as it had been set forth in his book *Il territorio dell'architettura* of 1966. Completely opposed to rendering buildings as freestanding objects, Gregotti regarded architectural form as the primary agent capable of contributing to the ever-evolving character of both land form and land use. In this respect he remained critical of any open-ended, instrumental exploitation of land. As he would remark in one of his more trenchant *Casabella* editorials:

> I believe that if there is a clear enemy to fight today, it is represented by the idea of an economic/technical space indifferent in all directions. This is now such a widespread idea that it seems almost objective. It seems to have gone a long way beyond the logic of profit to the point where it casts its ideological shadow even over the best intentions of public development in an exemplary alliance made up of bureaucratic thought, the power system and petit-bourgeois culture. . . . It is a question of a shrewd, modernistic enemy capable of accepting the latest, most fashionable proposal, especially any proposal capable of selling every vain formalistic disguise, favorable only to myth, redundancy or uproar, as a genuine difference.[1]

Gregotti was the first to recognize that it is the land itself that is at stake today rather than the traditional city. He came to see that the full crisis lay not only within the historical urban core but also in the ever-proliferating tentacles of the megalopolis, since it was these that were having the greatest cultural and physical impact, through the process of speculative subdivision and the wholesale consumption of agricultural land, not to mention the equally devastating abandonment of our obsolete industrial plants with all the negative ecological consequences that this entails. It is perhaps for these reasons that the "memory" of the site served as the mainspring of Gregotti's thought, since for him the geological and mythical history of the site was of as much consequence for its imminent development as the necessary recognition of its current use.

The other imperative for Gregotti was the need to take a "realistic" approach toward the production of built form, if for no other reason than to retain the architect's mastery over building production. For Gregotti, this whole aspect was to be subsumed (in both a pragmatic and poetic sense) under the term *technique,* although needless to say this invocation of the technical in a quasi-craft sense was not to be simplistically translated into universal technology. As he was to put it in another *Casabella* editorial:

> We have an exaggeratedly technical idea of technique (that marks out the productive aspects of the project instead of projection), whilst we tend to overshadow technique as a transformational guide, specific to architectural design. . . . Certainly design does not depend absolutely on technique; besides, there are never, nor have there ever been direct connections: technique is no longer a rational model of production nor the linguistic mimesis of its practices; however, since technique is the support of design ideas, the formation of meaning in architectural expression is in some way under its constant supervision

and guarantee. It is a matter of guaranteeing that the building enterprise does not turn into a loss but becomes a consolidation of the design. Such supervision is all the more necessary because building is no longer "a natural act" in any way, or even less linked to inhabitation. On the contrary it is undermined by uncertainties due to the habit of constantly starting anew to which design has been subjected for more than half a century.[2]

This dialogical habit of mind, which swerves unexpectedly as it moves from one level to the next, is characteristic not only of Gregotti's qualifying thought but also of his equally inflected practice. One might even say he is a builder rather than an architect, a Brunelleschi rather than an Alberti, and it is this ethos that has permeated *Casabella* throughout the fifteen years of his tenure as editor, a line sustained through insightful commentary and critique in one editorial after another. This stoic performance puts Gregotti in a class apart not only as an intellectual but also as an editor, since he has been one of the few editors in the field to assume the responsibility of writing a cogent column in every issue. Over the years these editorials have inevitably returned to the same set of themes, for all that the manner of broaching them has continually varied, the tack depending upon the content of the issue or the articulation of a particularly topical debate.

This continual reworking of a critical stance across a decade and a half has evidently served as the basis for this present volume, as one may judge from the itemized contents that treat sequentially projection, precision, technique, monumentality, and modification, to touch on only some of the key words that have preoccupied Gregotti over the years. In addition to these concerns, the first half of *Inside Architecture* has been devoted to the theme of conservation, with an emphasis upon its problematic relationship to modernization, particularly as this relates to the vast urban and territorial changes that have taken place in recent years. It is hard to imagine how this dilemma might be put more succinctly than in Gregotti's own words:

> It should be said that the resurgence of conservation has been greatly aided by the positive meaning that this word has recently assumed as a protector of architectural heritage, of nature, and of historical memory, in opposition to a modernization that demolishes and forgets. This originates largely from a widespread feeling of resistance to the domination of scientific thought, whose task is to continuously surpass the present: what has been done does not matter; what matters is to see what can be done. . . .
>
> Conservation invokes not only memory, but also the fact that the appearance of Picasso's painting does not make that of Poussin obsolete. In other words, conservation demands recognition for the share of eternity (although this expression is largely metaphorical) connected with the idea of artistic practice, as opposed to the essentially linear concept of progress—one that inevitably abandons its own past—common to all the natural sciences.[3]

Conservation is fundamentally opposed to the skeptical values of the postmodern world that for immediate gain is quite prepared to sacrifice the future as well as the past. This maximizing drive is to be distinguished from the unfinished modern project of the Frankfurt School that in criticizing its own processes puts into question any assumptions we may have adopted as to the necessary relations obtaining between reason and progress. This opposition between modernization and critical reason has now been further compounded by the rise of telematic communications and by the massification of the society through media, through what Max Horkheimer and Theodor Adorno long ago identified as the culture industry. That no one is quite immune to this homogenizing process is evidenced by Gregotti's subtle indictment of the way in which the architectural profession has been coopted by the commodifying values of the late modern world that are all the more insidious for being implied rather than declared. Thus we may recognize through Gregotti's characterization those aspects of contemporary practice that favor

> a little bit of modernity in techniques and communication; and perhaps a little tenor's high note here and there to add a touch of "artistry," especially in the form of inconsequential originality which introduces a shade of ineffability into the solution, an ineffability necessary for proving the existence of creative freedom. And above all a great deal of flexibility, which often results in close adherence to the folds of profit; a generous share of that plastic democracy that goes under the name of animation. . . . No definite form: rather, total plasticity and interchangeability of solutions within this context. In other words, no architecture.
>
> The solution is thus never the one that would suit the project and the place, one that would interpret

them according to some necessity. It is more likely
to be a solution already open to all hybridizations:
not the solution that, in its clarity, is able to include
and confront authentic differences, but rather a solution that tends to drown such differences in the
process of homogenization set in motion by diversity turned into pure ideology.[4]

This concern for authentic differences and for their articulation on many levels at once is the recitative that runs
throughout this identification of the aporias confronting contemporary practice in the last decade of the century. The author
believes that the modern project, irrespective of its scale and
scope, must assume the responsibility of criticizing the status
quo, together with its own contingency, rather than passively
accepting the brief or responding simplistically to a given
techno-economic demand. Nothing could be further from this
notion of the project as an act of critical transformation than the
supposedly "natural" linear process by which productive criteria come to be merged only too smoothly with the myth of
progress. In the face of this ideological elision critical practice
must be capable of synthesizing the necessary factors, without
flattening the macro and micro differences that are built into
the program or embodied within the site. Such an act of articulation is unavoidably opposed to any kind of pseudolinguistic
effect or to an artificial diversification "that lacks any actual diversity or significant conflict." Thus Gregotti's layered approach encourages one to discriminate between a whole range
of interconnected polarities, to wit pluralism versus populism,
monumentality versus monumentalism, technique versus technology, ornament versus decoration, manner versus caricature,
consistency versus homogenization and last but not least, when

it comes to legitimizing theoretical positions, between the description of a confusion and a confused description.

Echoing Alvaro Siza's aphorism that "architects don't invent anything, they transform reality," Gregotti asserts that the task of tectonic transformation involves confronting the rapacity of fashion and commodification while grounding the site in a literal sense, in order to endow the work with a feeling of historical depth. Given the thrust of multinational capitalism that oscillates between unmediated territorial exploitation and neglect, Gregotti is only too aware that such a call to arms can only be made in the name of a professional practice that would

> have none of the glorious characteristics of the great avant-gardes of the past. . . . It would be a patient minority, one able to consider duration without conceit, monuments without monumentalism; a minority capable of deep respect for skills and techniques, without the ideology of a craftsman's leather apron, and without any naive faith in the powers of hypermodern technological society; a minority able to take pleasure in free invention as the necessary solution to a question, not as frivolity. A minority whose acts would respect an economy of expressive means, as well as a simplicity achieved by passing through the complexities of reality without oversimplifying them; a minority capable of continuously constructing a critical distance from reality, above all from an overjustified context; a minority capable of rebuilding within itself the diversity required in a quest for clarity, but without undue pride over the momentary certainties that this produces; a minority

that wishes to remain outside of fashion and of image; a minority capable of returning materiality to the embodiment of things.[5]

Such a minority would be capable of restoring the value of parsimony implicit in the Latin term *praecisus*—meaning precision—without falling into reductive instrumentality. Thus the need at both a macro and a micro scale for the values of definition, measure, and corporeal integrity as these may be applied to the *earthwork* as much as to the *roofwork*. As the author is fond of saying, after Auguste Perret, "Il n'y a pas de détail dans la construction," meaning that even the smallest detail is crucial to the realization of the whole. Under this rubric ornamentation may only arise through a mutual synthesis of spatial and material articulation, that is to say, through a multiple inflection by which the program achieves an appropriate hierarchization of its parts.

Elsewhere Gregotti insists, after Louis Kahn, that monumentality is not a genre, that it is above all an aspiration for institutional durability rather than a rhetorical display of power; a concept best exemplified by the German word *Denkmal* that etymologically combines *denken,* to think, and *Mal,* time. On the other hand, as Gregotti ironically remarks: "If no value is given to the memory of past and present events, then there is no reason to build monuments for their future testimony. Nor would there be any reason to worry about the future existence of the value that we bring into being through the construction of architecture."[6]

As opposed to the stylistic superficialities of our time and the climate of opportunistic reform that suffuses the reactionary politics of the moment, Gregotti aligns himself with the prewar modern project in its most organic aspect, that is to say, with the "not yet" of Ernst Bloch—projected hope—as this must now address itself to the modification of land and the cultivation of the earth. He sees this going to ground, so to speak, as a cultural and ecological necessity, for, as he was to put it in 1983, the origins of architecture do not reside in the primitive hut but rather in a primordial marking of ground in order to delineate a human world against the unformed, chaotic indifference of the cosmos; in short, in the act of culture in the void of nature. This respect for primal symbiotic beginnings underlies Gregotti's categorical antipathy to the atopical typologies of the American strip, the supermarkets, parking lots, and service stations that permeate the ubiquitous megalopolis; tropes that, unlike the elements of the antique *extra muros,* are governed solely by the relentless processes of commodification and distribution. Against this "society of spectacle" that constantly strives to naturalize its existence, Gregotti posits a simplicity that is far from being natural, spontaneous, and dynamic. On the contrary it is rebarbative and complex. As he puts it, simplicity is neither a viable starting point nor an objective, for architecture is not *ipso facto* simple; it can only become simple.

As Lewis Mumford observed, the darker side of the information age resides in our incapacity to assimilate the unending proliferation of data that is placed at our disposal. While a great deal of such material is only of passing relevance, there can be no doubt that this continual flow has had a negative effect upon the overall quality of everyday production and hence has already prejudiced, as it were, the possibility of such input becoming culturally integrated into normative building form. The supposedly well-informed architect is often obliged to indulge in the consumerist trait of speed-reading, in which a text is read once and once only; a scanning reflex that one cannot fruitfully indulge in, in this particular instance. For this is a Socratic dialogue in which the architect talks unceasingly to his double, that is to say to his critical muse who weaves back and forth across the loom of the world, suspended between the intellectual refinement of an urban elite and the harsh confrontations of architectural practice.

This then is a summation of Gregotti's thought to date; an artificial anthology, as it were, that has been expressly compiled for an Anglo-American audience. As I have suggested, this is a text that demands to be read repeatedly; indeed it is hard to know how many times one might come to peruse it before exhausting its content, since here, more than in other essays of a similar genre, every sentence resonates with implications that escape the constraints of the format and thus provide a primer not only for an emerging theory of architecture but also for an immediate form of reflective practice.[7]

Kenneth Frampton

This translation is taken from Vittorio Gregotti's original edi-
tion of *Dentro l'architettura*, published by Bollati Boringhieri
in 1991. It is the most comprehensive of Gregotti's writings,
covering many of the themes that he investigated in his
monthly editorials for *Casabella*, the Italian journal that he directed from 1982 to 1996. It presents us with a candid view of
the discipline from within, citing its many problems and contradictions while also offering concise ways of reconstituting
its purpose and direction.

Certainly, Gregotti is writing in a time when there is
much to be questioned in architecture. He has approached this
debate cautiously, withholding any pretense of offering simple
answers to its problems. Instead, he is more inclined to be in-
ductive in his reasoning: examining the work of others, sifting
through critical discourse, and surveying the territory of other
disciplines before advancing any hypotheses. In the tradition of
Edoardo Persico and Giuseppe Pagano in the 1930s, or Ernesto
Rogers in the 1950s (all past editors of *Casabella*), Gregotti has
structured a means by which he can first understand urgent issues of the profession before acting upon them. Few contemporary architects have positioned themselves in this manner, and
Gregotti, with *Casabella* as his platform, has striven to circulate
such questions in a consistent and serious manner. It is therefore no surprise that we find *Inside Architecture* dedicated to a
further examination of what lies at the center of these questions, issues that help to redefine our position with respect to
modernity, and more specifically to the future prospects for an
architecture of modernism.

It is also significant that Gregotti has enriched his discourse by engaging in a substantial professional practice. Gregotti Associati, established in 1974, has designed, planned, and built projects both in Italy and abroad. Few architects today, with the possible exception of Alan Colquhoun, can claim to have profoundly influenced the discipline as both practicing architects and critical writers. Of course, many have annotated built works of others in order to announce coming trends, or have published colorful monographs and collected works that clear alternative paths to follow. But although such displays may offer temporary relief from the anxieties that plague us, seldom do they have any lasting effects within the discipline.

Gregotti is quite suspicious of those critics and architects who isolate themselves from the specific environmental and social context of an architectural project. He is equally troubled by those who disregard the traditions of architectural culture itself. Instead, he seeks to understand and modify the specific situations that confront theory within a project, while simultaneously engaging in the specialized activities of construction through a grounded relationship with its own traditions. Such a perspective involves not only constructing critical ideas, but also dismantling built work in order to generate alternative concepts. On this note we can better understand why Gregotti structures *Inside Architecture* in two distinct parts: one addressing critical questions that encourage reflection on the reasons behind our projects, and one outlining the motives and mechanisms that drive the activities involved in project-making itself.

Many of the book's themes are shaped by Gregotti's concerns about contemporary conservatism, and specifically about works promoted by architects who have attempted to reject the modern project in favor of past architectures and the sentiments of historical memory. Some might argue that we have passed beyond such interests, and that we are now wiser and better equipped to address the actual problems of architecture and culture (for example, those that advocate renewed interest in the avant-garde, or experiment with techno-popular imagery). But the flood of historical sentiment has not necessarily subsided; on the contrary, it seems to have spread well beyond architectural circles. Clearly, the damage we see in today's urban environment stems less from the nostalgia of architects who championed such imagery fifteen years ago than from the aftershock of second-order designers, developers, and speculators who continue to market such illusions to the general public. In Gregotti's view, this market-driven wave has led to a "homogenization" of architectural culture, a kind of "hypermodernism" that resists any alternative representations. He also remains doubtful that more recent trends will be able to evade this problem, simply because they rely on the same market mechanisms to disseminate their images. It is only a matter of time before these experiments suffer a similar fate at the hands of second-rate promoters.

These concerns inform Gregotti's desire to clarify the specific nature of modern thought in contemporary architecture. As he explains it, although the idea of modernism has been criticized as a unitary process, a rigid ideology, or an appeal to the myth of progress, in fact these traits are more stereotypical than real. The modern movement of this century has included several lines of thought, at times conflicting; it accepts its own limits while simultaneously questioning the interdisciplinary agents that define these limits. An architectural project of modernity is "a new thing that moves, interprets, and reorganizes the overall system" of what is known; it should be recognized as a mode of working rather than as a form.[1] The task of modernity, argues Gregotti, is therefore to establish difference: not the kind of difference that frees architecture from any established historical memory or scientific development, and not a difference that attempts to defer meaning linguistically, but rather one that organizes the conflicts of a situation by functioning as a critical instrument for examining what already exists.

With this description, Gregotti attempts to re-form the concept of modernity, drawing on its earlier meaning. As Jürgen Habermas has noted, prior to the Enlightenment "to be modern" was a mode that allowed new epochs to form themselves through a changing relationship with past traditions. Following this period a new view of modernism arose, one that sought to sever all ties with the classical in order to advance new trends. This led in part to a culture of bourgeois aesthetic appeal, where any single artistic achievement could only exist through a cycling, novelty-driven relationship with other more stylish ideas that would subsequently replace it.[2]

Gregotti acknowledges that recent architectural efforts have attempted to reconnect with past traditions, but while "attempts to find legitimation in traditions and history ought to be the main weapons of conservation; instead, they are often a product of the hypermodern transience that generated and then overturned them through transforming the very concept of transience into a myth, which also became a cyclical reconstruction of many traditions."[3] Though well intentioned, the failure of these attempts have left recent architectural productions exposed to future eradication by the next new canon that is certain to replace them.

In his 1923 introduction to Baudelaire's *Tableaux parisiens,* Walter Benjamin tells us that when literary works are translated, the success of the result depends on the "translatability" of the original. Even though a translation may fail to reproduce the precise significance of the earlier work, it nevertheless assumes an "afterlife" that moves the essence of the original into a new context. A translation thus involves more than repeating information; it establishes a "kinship" to its previous form that does not rely on simple imitation.[4] For Gregotti, a renewed sense of the modern project would assume such a mode. Like the translation, the project must actively acknowledge existing situations and patterns so that their essences remain readable without becoming sentimental or nostalgic. In this view, architectural project-making becomes a creative activity that seizes ideas and materials that appear to be worn out and then rewrites them into a situation that allows for further maturation.

Some may question whether Gregotti's ideas can be effectively translated to our situation in the United States, where architectural traditions may seem too shallow to muster any significance comparable to that of their European counterparts. Yet this is where *Inside Architecture* reads most urgently, since it questions, by virtue of the modern project, many attitudes that originated in this country, reflecting on the conditions of our own modern predicament.

I would like to thank The University of North Carolina at Charlotte and its College of Architecture for providing essential funding and support for this project. Special mention should go to my colleague Francesca Zaccheo for her excellent work on the initial translation. I would also like to thank Kenneth Frampton, Joseph Rykwert, and Roger Conover for their enthusiastic encouragement, and in particular Pamela Grundy, whose dedicated editing efforts proved essential to its realization.

Peter Wong

ACKNOWLEDGMENTS

Many are the intellectual debts that this book must acknowledge; many are the friends with whom I have discussed varying aspects of its contents. I must at least name Salvatore Veca and Bernardo Secchi who have indulgently reviewed this work, and the editors of the magazine *Casabella,* where some of these writings have appeared in slightly different form. Many of my arguments have been discussed with them, as well as with the young (and less young) architects who work with me on a daily basis.

A special thanks to Antonella Bergamin, who with infinite patience has retyped this text many times.

Finally, to Marina, to whom I owe the title of this volume.

Vittorio Gregotti

INSIDE ARCHITECTURE

This book consists of two parts, which differ in the way questions are posed rather than in contents or materials, and which reflect two symmetrical, equally architectural points of view.

The first part considers some of the conditions surrounding current developments in architectural discourse. Since I am convinced that empirical conditions provide essential material for the artistic practice of our discipline, I consider a discussion of the hierarchy, the nature, and the significance of such conditions to be highly important for architecture.

Some possible ways to use these conditions in the architectural project are discussed in the second part of this book. These methods have been chosen and treated in fragmentary form, as pieces of possible design procedures, but although they do not claim to form a complete theory of architecture today, they do at least present a particular point of view.

Many of the questions that I consider as conditions for a project in the first half of this book become protagonists, as procedures, in the second. There, I describe how conjunctions, disjunctions, and hierarchies place the various materials in an organized and essential relationship with purpose and place, coming together to form an architectural project.

The second half of this book might thus be seen as the enumeration and description of a discontinuous series of design acts that I believe to be significant in the present debate, also from the perspective of their underlying exclusions.

The first part of the book takes the form of a continuous discourse. It proposes a series of connections, including some with issues that other disciplines have considered with much greater authority. Here, I attempt to present these issues from the point of view of architecture and its dilemmas. The ambiguous notion of conservation runs through the entire first half, which presents its reasons, advantages, and many contradictions in relation to new interpretations and discussions revolving around the theme of modernity.

This part attempts to look beyond the self-legitimizing discussion recently carried on in architectural circles, often in cannibalistic fashion. It proposes to revisit the uneven and uncertain terrain of values and objects that make up the reality against which, beyond which, or for which design projects are formed. Obviously, this return does not seek to approve or justify; rather, the terrain becomes a subject of architectural critique, a starting point for a possible architectural project for understanding and rearranging the present.

The second part, where I consider issues of design practice, also serves to distinguish the significant actions pertaining to our discipline, including the most imaginative, from those belonging to other artistic endeavors.

In the architectural project, the complicated involvement of diverse and often culturally distinct creative forces, as well as the system by which construction information is communicated and the considerable time employed in development and realization, all come together to establish a unique need to produce transformations, within limits that must be known, suffered, and utilized in the project's formation. In fact, I find it impossible to consider my discipline a mere representation of, or a peripheral writing about, what is already there.

Moreover, the issues raised by today's large urban and territorial interventions, as well as by solutions employed for smaller, even minute, strategic modifications, require a talent for mastering complex issues, which include relationships between fields of expertise and the critical limits of their respective roles, as well as the all-important effort to lay the groundwork for specific projects. Perhaps this is, for architecture, one of the most exhausting, intriguing, and inevitable conditions of our time.

All this should not involve transforming architects into managers or cultural organizers, and certainly not converting them into political racketeers. On the contrary, it involves resisting our expulsion (or self-exclusion, by taking on a purely decorative role) from our own universe of specific expertise, traditionally called upon to give meaningful form to the available techniques for transforming the physical world.

These writings take a form that might a bit pompously be defined as theoretical reflection. This is not a choice but a necessity for our projects. It is not directed against talent; rather, I believe it is an indispensable condition for the cultivation of talent. Many have pointed out how difficult it is to find a suitable platform for the issue of theory that serves our specific problems as effectively as did architectural treatises of the past. Until now, we have failed at this task, and our theoretical reflections have often become a subspecies of philosophy or a simplification of historical or epistemological thought. At some times, such reflections serve as *a posteriori* justification for architectural work. At others, they produce a metaphoric interference between different languages that instead need to maintain open but clear identities in order to communicate.

But this does not mean the problem of theory does not exist. Within the complicated geography of the feeble positions of recent years, it has been easy to surrender to the fatalism of fragmentation, seeing in it a portrait of the infinitely open interpretations that characterize the disorder of our consciousness, or to react against it by espousing a totally imaginary order.

In spite of the much-discussed crisis of the intellectual, I believe it is more important than ever for today's project to practice the highest possible level of critical reason, which even with its well-known limits should be considered suitable material for construction. This matters also because only critical reason makes it possible to continue with the modern project, to whose incompleteness I here expose myself entirely.

The paths of artistic practice have become decidedly conservative in recent years, whether they have involved retracing the roads of myth and symbol, or, more simply, the praise of common sense, or a wish to reconquer the languages and abilities of the profession and find in them a refuge from uncertainties while at the same time demanding recognition for the rights and seriousness of well-done work. Representation, description, and imitation are receiving close attention again, and many different efforts are seeking to reconnect the threads of every rhetorical tradition. In short, most recent artistic productions of any value display a wish to discard linguistic experiments or structural radicalisms, distancing themselves from any form of avant-garde program.

It should be said that the resurgence of conservation has been greatly aided by the positive meaning that this word has recently assumed as a protector of architectural heritage, of nature, and of historical memory, in opposition to a modernization that demolishes and forgets. This originates largely from a widespread feeling of resistance to the domination of scientific thought, whose task is to continuously surpass the present: what has been done does not matter; what matters is to see what can be done. As Paolo Rossi wrote, to become outdated is for scientific thought not just a destiny but a goal.[1]

Conservation invokes not only memory, but also the fact that the appearance of Picasso's painting does not make that of Poussin obsolete. In other words, conservation demands recognition for the share of eternity (although this expression is largely metaphorical) connected with the idea of artistic practice, as opposed to the essentially linear concept of progress—one that inevitably abandons its own past—common to all the natural sciences.

Thus in some ways the conservative attitude also invokes the history that joins the human sciences (although this classification has become rather blurred) to tradition and its incessant recovery and reinterpretation.

All this thus has its reasons, but one must understand that these reasons are complex and intrinsically contradictory, especially in relation to the apparent aspirations of the present hypermodern organization of society: an arrangement that strives to eliminate boundaries between the sciences, to be open, anti-ideological, infinitely interpretable and combinable, and above all to avoid horizons and long-term hopes, because they are considered illusions for which it is not worth sacrificing anything of the immediately acquirable.

From this point of view some claim that the crisis of what has been called the modern project, in its comprehensive cultural effort to deal with society rather than belief, is essentially the crisis of an illusion that joins hope and deception, against which it is therefore legitimate to respond, whether with hypermodern or with conservative attitudes.

Some say that this illusion stems mainly from a mistaken belief in the existence of a unitary historical process with definite ends (or one that can be reconstructed as such), combined with the belief that the creative process can encompass movements toward or against this history while remaining connected to it.

But as we know, the discussion regarding the decline of the idea of a unitary historical process started more than a century ago, and it has thus paralleled the formation of modern visual and architectural culture, which itself embodies many aspects of this crisis. It is precisely this discussion, with its groping toward universalism and its critique of established genres, that has helped to destroy the possibility of interpreting the history of culture in a linear and Eurocentric fashion.

But although this ongoing critique has always formed an integral part of the principles of modernity, it has never prevented a continuous production of "histories," albeit according to varying historical hypotheses or to methods that had the partiality of their own interpretations as a central premise. Nor has it prevented the construction of architectures that sprang from a decidedly unitary idea of utopia, while featuring a plurality of interpretations for the very idea of modernity.

In particular, the plurality of modern experience in the specific case of architecture—that is, the existence of several complex lines within the "modern movement"—has been widely discussed ever since the fifties, when it became evident that what had once appeared as a common basis for a modern front was gradually weakening. This discussion also stemmed from the growing difficulty of any legitimating symbolic appeal, including the appeal to the myth of progress as a process of liberation and rationality, which had accompanied the rise of the idea that modernity was a value in itself.

I believe this to be the contradictory but central aspect of the modern age, with which it becomes possible to overturn the current judgment of rigidity and ideological self-limitation that conservatives and hypermodernists have pronounced against modernity. The modern project critiques society rather than forming a natural part of it; that is, it is able to question both the limits of its own arrangement and the relationship between reason and progress. Thus, it encourages the very questions about the unity of history, systems, and ends that have been presented as the illusions of modernity.

Such questions also raise the possibility of becoming lost in the labyrinth of contradictions opened by critical thought. But that is a different issue, one that inspires neoconservative thought, which imagines it can combat this danger by resorting to the self-discipline contained in the aesthetic norms of tradition.

The modern project contains instead the positive illusion of being able to formulate hypotheses with a clear awareness of their specific limits.

With modernity, we have thus already spent a century in the age of transformation and contradiction, and I believe this is demonstrated by the best architectural productions of the past hundred years.

This should not, however, mean entering an age of total subservience to the interchangeability of interpretations or of indifferent substitutions; it should not imply transforming critical thought into a mere instrument of variation within the overwhelming homogeneity that runs through culture and society.

 MASS HOMOGENEITY

The hypermodernists' argument against modernity states that architecture's goal should no longer be the constitution of critical tension, but rather a natural relationship with the tastes of the masses. On the contrary, I believe such taste moves toward the illusion of liberty that accompanies the idea of infinite flexibility, and consequently toward an absence of forms and horizons. This involves an elevation of the illusory private sphere, which is being extended to public action as a kind of aesthetic of stylistic familiarity—an illusion of identity and belonging that transforms all things into folklore or quaintness, experienced as a supposed antidote against the anonymity of the power that guides it in an intimate solidarity of culture and aims.

The polemic against the reputed ability of art to propose uncomfortable alternatives has also been insistently revisited, using old and inadequate arguments that not even a subtle thinker like Feyerabend escapes:

> Religion, sciences, technologies, and art—says the philosopher—carry the seeds of megalomania within them: when given unlimited power, they become tyrannical. For example our cities where urban planners and architects can do and undo at will, without ever asking the inhabitants whether they like what might forever remain under their noses.[2]

Unlimited power is something that architects and urban planners certainly have less and less of. But more importantly, Feyerabend here underestimates the fact that if his judgment were radicalized, it would probably lead to the disappearance not only of the entire history of architecture, but also of all of the cultural critiques of minorities and opposition groups, and thus the whole of modern culture. I do not think that is what he desires.

At this point we should remember Adorno's famous words, when he spoke about functionalism at the inauguration of the Deutscher Werkbund in 1965: "Architecture worthy of human beings thinks better of men than they actually are." He continued by saying:

Things are not universally correct in architecture and universally incorrect in men. Men suffer enough injustice, for their consciousness and unconsciousness are trapped in a state of minority; they have not, so to speak, come of age. This nonage hinders their identification with their own concerns. Because architecture is in fact both autonomous and purpose-oriented, it cannot simply negate men as they are. And yet it must do precisely that if it is to remain autonomous.[3]

After almost two centuries of merging creativity and critical conscience as the basis for modernity, it is important to emphasize the present attempt by hypermodern culture to render architectural culture (and not only architectural culture) homogeneous with the social order. It is an imposing and highly significant attempt from which neoconservative creative thought mistakenly believes it can escape by founding its instruments on past traditions of order, hierarchies, and contrasts. Meanwhile, dialectical tension seems to have been lost forever in the triumph of the freedom without horizons found in mass behavior.

In other words, what guides choices as far as architecture is concerned, especially the choices of public institutions, is a form of neofunctionalism that caters to mass behavior, in which the present state of democracy is supposedly represented.

There is an entire body of literature that attempts to describe the behavior of crowds as following very different laws than that of individuals: one needs simply to read a few masterful pieces by Elias Canetti to profoundly grasp that difference.[4] But could it be that today this difference is collapsing to the point that individual behavior, moved by opportunism or the pressure of communication, is starting to coincide with mass behavior?

And what sort of architectural project has been devised to answer the critiques raised by hypermodernists and conservatives?

It is a rather complicated and heterogeneous mixture, elaborated through the collaboration of architects themselves: a little bit of context, but in its most insensitive quantitative or stylistic interpretation; a little bit of modernity in techniques and communication; and perhaps a little tenor's high note here and there to add a touch of "artistry," especially in the form of inconsequential originality which introduces a shade of ineffability into the solution, an ineffability necessary for proving the existence of creative freedom. And above all a great deal of flexibility, which often results in close adherence to the folds of profit; a generous share of that plastic democracy that goes under the name of animation; a dash of inconsequential participationalism. All this is seasoned with a few drops of environmentalist fundamentalism. No definite form: rather, total plasticity and interchangeability of solutions within this context. In other words, no architecture.

The solution is thus never the one that would suit the project and the place, one that would interpret them according to some necessity. It is more likely to be a solution already open to all hybridizations: not the solution that, in its clarity, is able to include and confront authentic differences, but rather a solution that tends to drown such differences in the process of homogenization set in motion by diversity turned into pure ideology.

The ideas and principles that the best part of the modern tradition has striven to put forward in recent years, which include the principles of contextual relationship, of modification, of belonging, and of limited and specific research, are being used to this end, mixed together with the worst remains of rational functionalism, with the aestheticism of memory (rather than its deep levels of priceless discourse), as well as with the exhibitionistic style of techniques.

If we, moreover, examine even the most glorified aspects of contemporary production, what seems to await us on the other shore, full of creative poverty and unblessed by irony, is the reductionism of the most recent architectural monumentalisms, which attempt to directly represent the junction of powers and techniques, or the architectural metaphor of undue deconstructivist transposition, which represents an attempt to remove all referential content. Together, these reduce architecture to mere decoration.

The fundamental architectural principle of consistency, including consistency between parts, between the exterior and the interior, between content, subject, and meaning, between form and construction, is lost. Even the value of a deliberate inconsistency is lost. The ground for neoconservative positions is thus perfectly prepared and their arrival imminent.

Often today the principle of consistency has become a race toward vulgar practicality (and it seems to me that architectural culture, following the period of refusing professional praxis in the name of the purity of self-referential design, is quickly becoming overly practical). But even where this has not occurred, the idea of consistency appears to be leaning toward such an extreme generalization of functional relationships that it deprives them of the material resistance of aims, techniques, and site, which the project ought to encounter, discuss, and organize.

Without that material resistance, the organization of a project inevitably remains a prisoner of pure market competition and of the narrow range allowed by the relative oscillations of communication, which seem to have ever more rigidly fixed boundaries. Consistency is thus again transformed into something resembling the homogenization of aspirations, language, and behavior. Such homogenization deprives architectural construction of all commitments to alternative representations, except for the temporary originality required by the market. Consistency between practice and theory in architectural form thus comes to be seen as a useless restriction on the apparently decisive aesthetic rules of the novelty of images, or as a mere aid to the goal of being recognized by the market, accepted in its total ineffability.

From this standpoint, the current stylistic fragmentation of architectural positions appears consistent with a condition of diversification that lacks any actual diversity or significant conflict. Such are the results of the homogenization and progressive reabsorption of architectural culture into an architecture that forms a perversely organic part of the portrait of social behaviors.

———————————— In Defense ————————————

All this is happening in the foreground of yet another difficulty. Today, the dynamics of economic and social systems offer an important (though very unstable) series of great opportunities for physically transforming the environment, while at the same time they are unable to offer any grand horizons for ideals. Meanwhile, for the reasons explained above, architecture is unable to produce any broad organizational inventions or alternative hypotheses.

It is enough to consider how some themes, developed recently with great vigor, have thus far produced mere traces of any convincing answers. The past twenty-five years, for example, have witnessed insistent talk about issues related to the designability of landscapes, which is considered an innovation for projects on all scales. Undoubtedly, the issue of the historicity of the natural, or the relationship between processes of structural transformation and their aesthetic incorporation, or the contrasts of the internationalization of image-making and production techniques with the idea of place, have all been more effectively discussed in the past few years. But in reality, the notion of landscape has been internally eroded by a blind, frenetic occupation of space, and the neonaturalism that opposes this process is just as harmful to any human idea of landscape. Assimilation, integration, and nostalgia seem to be the only criteria capable of opposing the scattered dispersion and the complete atopicality of interventions, and such opposition is relatively limited.

The same can be said about urban design, which is barely held in check by a weak conscience that attempts to oppose or to reconcile with contextual conditions but never engages them in dialogue. Its most frequent sources of inspiration involve a return to entrenched rules of recomposition, which seem to be the only rules that can present us with the illusion of a great historical tradition and the idea of regulating the current growth of cities. Other inspirations resort to representing the fragmentation of contemporary thought through the fragmentation of form, to the point that the architecture of cities dissolves into communicative immateriality.

Perhaps consistent with conditions dictated by the majority class is the view of cities and territories as collections of independent technical or stylistic objects, a view that accepts processes of economic and image exploitation as conditions without alternatives, and only considers quality as a sum of the individual talents that happen to participate.

Moreover, due to the fragmented divergence of techniques, cultures, horizons, and specialized languages, each step in the realization of a project reveals itself as a fatal betrayal of the principles (weak as they may be) that one has managed to set in motion. At times, the haste and the size of productions lead to an excessive reduction of the rich articulations we have learned from tradition. In contrast with the gradual stratification of historical cities, this need to eliminate all accidents is systematically revealed in the form of inconsistency, or artificially decorative variation, and at times even through imitation of the historical process.

Naturally, this portrayal is consistently negative only in potential. Anyone working in the field of architecture can list numerous incongruities in systems, and thus also the many transformations that might be conceived from the standpoint of the inconsistent homogeneity of the system.

Critical thought is free to express itself, but it has been reduced (or has reduced itself) to superfluity. Therefore, we often face a somewhat contradictory situation: that of working toward the modernization of technologies, institutions, modes of production, and processes of planning and communication, while simultaneously thinking of these procedures as bound to a quality that denies any effort of modernization to take possession of the very principle of quality.

Thus, one is increasingly restricted to a form of literary resistance based on the limits of a specific subject and its self-referential affirmation, while renouncing any attempt to use the discipline's instruments to describe reality anew.

Even those who try to think of specificity as a new beginning, as a reaffirmation of the primal reasons at the essence of our discipline, are partly mired in this tendency. I do not refer to the recurrent discussions regarding the primitive hut and the origins of architecture, which appear in every ancient treatise and whose history has been masterfully described in Joseph Rykwert's book *On Adam's House in Paradise*.[5] I would rather, to paraphrase Husserl in "The Origin of Geometry," attempt to recover the original meaning of the architecture that was handed down and that continued to have value and to be reshaped while still remaining architecture in all its incarnations: this in order to understand the extent to which this might renew our sense of what to do.[6]

In the present situation, such research into original intentions seems important but remains difficult to practice, because it requires a firmness of purpose that I believe we can neither conceive nor apply.

For us, the issue is the more modest one of constructing some trace of a foundation for an architecture useful to the defense and rearrangement of the present, and also (fatally, from this standpoint) oriented more toward conservation and restitution than toward any future program.

Fortunately, the way that such a defense functions—that is, the way the project is used as conservation and restitution—forms the crucial element that distinguishes it from pure nostalgia and avoids confusion between conservation and conservatism. The space available to it seems to consist of a congenital imperfection regarding this aim; that is, of a deviation from the idea of conservation and resistance that presents itself as an immeasurable distance. I believe that to inhabit this distance, to choose it as one's place of action, is also the only way to maintain the firm, in some ways hostile, character that marks the tradition of the modern creative project. Its different, oppositional appearance is practiced not out of an intentional or loquaciously subjective bizarreness, but as a logical need in view of the existing conditions, a difference that represents the only kind of common sense that can be practiced.

On the other hand, while the architectural project needs great freedom of thought and expression, it does not require absolute freedom of conditions. Rather, such conditions represent a resistant, irreplaceable material to be criticized and molded by the project itself. My fear is that the articulation and specificity of this material is gradually becoming conventional, assuming the form of a tacitly conditioned freedom that makes it impossible to establish any authentic difference.

I believe that the artistic practice of architecture instead involves an obligation to look at the empirical world in order to modify it, overturn it, and deny it, but also to open a critical dialogue with it. This is perhaps an inopportune dialogue, but one that can penetrate the cracks of this world in order to confront and modify it.

A designer must conceive hypotheses with a passion for the absolute, but also an awareness of their temporary status. It is the awareness of one's own marginality (and sometimes the inability of institutions to recognize the threat posed by this marginal status) that has allowed many modern works to be conceived and realized as forms that *must be*.

Instead, there are some, like Gianni Vattimo, who hold that the "ornamental essence of the culture of mass society, the ephemeral quality of its products, the eclecticism by which it is dominated, the impossibility of identifying anything essential . . . fully corresponds to the *Wesen* of the aesthetic in late modernity."[7]

Many of the symptoms that I have attempted to describe above undoubtedly converge toward this judgment; however, I cannot recognize any element of this situation that allows us to see some noble survival of architecture in it, even though I do realize that the idea of nobility is, today, a very weak argument.

The reasons behind some of the present neoconservative attitudes also have their roots in such questions, but without providing any convincing answers: the absence of any foundation prevents both a breakthrough toward the future and a creative organization of the present. In other words, this condition seems to resist solution either by the new, which lacks the support of any founding tension and thus takes the purely bizarre form of being different, or by the attempt at radical rethinking which, in turn, is absorbed into the catalogue of the "transitional new." Nor is it possible to resort to memories and traditions, because without any project for the present these merely become a nostalgia for some kind of legitimation.

It is also evident that inside our discipline, more than thirty years of critiquing modern architecture (a necessary and difficult critique that started here in Italy in the early fifties) have led to a series of conclusions that have failed to reconstruct any structure of horizons and perspectives, or even any consistent renewal of instruments or methods.

Wider links have been drawn between the different moments of modernity, clarifying the reasons behind its internal oppositions and tracing the modern tradition all the way back to its origins in the crisis of classicism. That which exists has begun to be considered a value in itself, leading to a concept of the project as a dialogue with the historical geography of the context. As a result, the concepts of novelty, imitation, function, essence, meaning, and modification have become active elements within the project. But all this has led to no convincing, universal arguments capable of proposing authentic alternatives.

The main issue, however, has involved setting in motion some principles relevant to the constitution of new hierarchies among project materials with respect to the traditional hierarchies of modernism. If reconsidered with enough prudence and balance, an emphasis on these principles might make possible an architecture that would avoid the coarsest errors dictated by professional subservience, or the frenzies that presently replace the authenticity of a poetic profession. But it would certainly not be true to say that all this has led to the constitution of general rules, glorious and durable enough to construct great architecture.

It is this approximation, this rush to take possession of the latest fashion, this productivistic superficiality, that makes it possible to say that the general trait that best characterizes the architecture of these times is not mannerism but caricature, and primarily self-caricature. This expressive category is, of course, absolutely unsuited to our discipline.

First of all, elements of caricature are drawn from the modernist tradition, which is viewed as "that pretty style from the twenties." Or they are hurled against it formally, whether through borrowing from the tradition of the grotesque or through quoting material without any understanding of its sense or origin, a process that involuntarily creates the exaggeration, the overcharging of meanings and their warping with respect to signs, and the heavy makeup and accentuation of features that often lie at the heart of caricature.

A desire to draw away from this condition, albeit without pointing to any authentic alternative, provides another reason for neoconservative research, which recognizes the features of an absolutely untenable condition of neurotic precariousness.

An important aspect of the present conservative attitude derives precisely from a reaction to this elevation of precariousness into ideology.

The nostalgia for a rule, if not for some aesthetic norm, reappears as a wish to slow down action in order to reflect, a wish to see the work develop slowly and to keep it under control, a desire for solidity and durability of construction.

On the other hand, in view of the crisis of any horizon of meaning that is not opportunistic or cynical, it becomes obvious that the search for a foundation of architectural activity can take the deceptive direction of a return to the individual traditions of the discipline, primarily that of reexamining the capabilities of specific instruments. This strategy focuses above all on a return to professional skills, including the aspect of craftsmanship, and can even involve revitalizing old ideas of dividing the discipline into genres and specifics.

But as far as architecture is concerned, this search should first proceed through a radical rethinking of the notion of the project, which modernity has transformed into the idea of an autonomous productive cycle that embraces numerous human activities, and which is essential for ensuring a complete prevision of the work, as well as of the process by which it will be realized.

In the past half-century, the notion of the architectural project has been the subject of particularly active reflection. This critique (I am thinking especially of Massimo Cacciari) emphasizes the alliance forged over the past two centuries between the words "project," "production," and "progress."[8] This alliance has opposed the other meaning of the word "project," which stresses projection, fervor, tearing away from a situation in order to criticize, deconstruct, and question it; essentially, the idea of freeing oneself from presupposition in order to construct a new understanding, or even a new ontological constitution.

According to this second meaning, project-making in architecture could never be a mere matter of techniques and instruments, but would simultaneously construct a critique of the present and of the horizon of its reorganization.

Thus, the notion of project oscillates between the opposing meanings of domination and liberation, of control and unfolding of differences, of prevision and prediction, of opening toward what might emerge and planning for it.

The process of constructing architecture through a project can, therefore, be considered a quite specific way of thinking. The main difficulty in describing its distinctive and specific features arises from a constant participation by sources of knowledge and ways of thought that differ from and sometimes oppose each other in their references and levels. Examples would be scientific observation, sympathetic understanding, inspirations, tradition, memory, and so forth.

Moreover, scientific and technical thought, with all its increasing importance, has for many years emphasized the value of hypotheses, of conjectures temporarily suited to resolving and explaining a group of problems, and this has certainly brought scientific and creative procedures closer to each other through their analogous forms of interactive and diagonal thought.

In general, as we know, scientific rationality has affected this century's creative procedures in important ways, as both a formal and a methodological model.

This reasoning leads us to regard an architectural fact as also a problem of knowledge. It becomes less a collection of empirical elements for construction, and more a new thing that moves, interprets, and reorganizes the overall system and theory of knowledge. Still, knowledge is not in the forefront as the central problem of architecture, nor does it define any specific approach.

In architectural processes, the various forms of thought that I have described above seem to remain suspended, like particles that are mixed together but whose diversity can still be recognized. One might suggest that it is this oscillation of nonhomogeneous methods that forms the specific nature of project-making thought in architecture, or even propose that the prevalence of one of these elements over the others—or, more specifically, a varying hierarchy among them—can furnish material for a diversity of architectural solutions.

Still, it is clear that this explanation provides only a negative answer to questions about the specifics of project-oriented thought.

Of course, we might consider the special type of thought that forms the construction of an architectural project solely from the standpoint of the "task of establishing difference." But I believe that although this might be possible for other creative disciplines, architecture carries firmly inscribed within itself the conditions for constructing something that in no way exists at the starting point of present materials, aims, sites, techniques, and conditions.

As we know, some interpretations tend to see the notion of difference not simply as a liberation from historical time, and from the will of science and technology, but as the very foundation of a conscience able to see diversity as necessary.

But this does not mean "a conscience freed from being useful," or freed from all confrontation with empirical experience; it means an attempt to clarify and describe the conflicts of the present condition. It is true that in order to be transformed into a project such a description must indeed make itself into a foundation for difference, but without presuming to propose that this difference represents a definitive way out of such conflicts.

Thus, the foundation of difference is not simply an attempt to escape from this time of precariousness and poverty, nor is it a proposal for global rationality, which cannot be found today in any form. Rather, the value of difference appears in the creative process above all as a defense of its own possible conception through the intervention of critical reason in what exists.

Returning directly (and perhaps illegitimately) to the question of architecture, this means that the foundation of difference is neither the new, with its presumption of a new beginning, nor an aesthetic utopia, but rather a condition that enables architecture to speak a limited and specific truth.

In other words, I believe that the foundation of architecture and its project are possible only if both the language of announcement and that of technical-scientific possession are abandoned, in favor of deciphering, listening, and critical construction.

Evidently, these reflections seem to suppress any connotation of the project as simply an answer to what exists, abandoned to the fatality of its existence, or as determination and prevision of the future (or perhaps even as a prediction; that is, stabilizing discontinuous points of reference by means of the architectural object). As we shall see further on, prevision and prediction are possible forms of two aspects of production, which start from a certain condition and then tear away from it.

In hypermodern ideology, instead, the notion of the project's aspects of possession, announcement, and the foundation of difference seems to be a prisoner of the present, both in "that ornamental essence of culture" mentioned above and in the infinite interpretability of that same essence, from which, I realize, even this piece of writing itself is not exempt.

But if this were a wholly real condition, the question of the modalities of architectural action would have to be restricted to simple contingencies, and thus to possibility and chance—in fact, to all possibilities and chances.

As the preeminent material and central content of the project, contingency would then claim to represent the specific nature of the project procedure, open to any kind of reason or knowledge, as long as it does not form any horizon or conclusion for the case in question.

Architecture reacts to this situation by taking a conservative direction, by searching for some foundation, sometimes an illusion, sometimes one based on the illusory aesthetic security of tradition and historical legitimation. But since the very traditions on which principles, models, and ideologies are founded have gradually been losing their ability to construct orders that transcend individual events, specific conditions are increasingly emerging as the only possible elements on which to base a project.

Attempts to find legitimation in traditions and history ought to be the main weapons of conservation; instead, they are often a product of the hypermodern transience that generated and then overturned them through transforming the very concept of transience into a myth, which also became a cyclical reconstruction of many traditions. On the other hand, specific conditions have also often come to simulate reality and necessity, reducing the project to a simple response that cannot avoid fishing for the images of its own creation amid the by now crowded and interchangeable system that has been crammed with the rules and symbols of those same traditions.

At this point, the subject that I have (perhaps improperly) called critical reason returns to the surface. This is a highly contractual kind of critical reason, which plays an irreplaceable role in forming a filter that can avert the possibility of anything at all entering into any project whatsoever, thus crowding out the sense and necessity of specific truth.

This critical reason involves the ability to define this question profoundly enough to formulate hypotheses regarding the essence of the transformative relationships that it induces. The presence of these transformative elements then becomes the presence of the surrounding empirical world, that irreplaceable material within which we establish the space to be filled in by architecture. The quality of the architecture then rests on the depth of examination and articulation of that space.

—————————————— PREVISION, PREDICTION ——————————————

But the shape of that space is also defined by the ways in which possible previsions, based on interpretations of the specific situation, intersect not only with collective inclinations and expectations, but also with the ways that such previsions are arranged in varying disciplines: economic, productive, sociological, demographic, and so on.

It therefore becomes necessary to find an architectural incarnation for such previsions and expectations, to reach an agreement on the timing of prevision by the rhythms of different disciplines, and to seek a point of agreement on the duration, speed, and acceleration of such varying previsions. We know that in the past, and also (we imagine) in the future, the changes of various disciplines do not follow a constant rhythm, but are subject to accelerations and arrests that occur in irregular patterns. The division of time with respect to these varying previsions thus presents an irregular surface, where certain issues have experienced sudden surges and setbacks while others have moved more slowly and regularly.

But what place does prevision occupy within the hierarchies of the architectural process, and most importantly, to what extent does prevision participate in the cautious element: that is, in the form of thought that measures before leaping? In other words, to what extent does prevision clash with the idea of prediction, which is the central content of the architectural project, the authentic form of diversification?

I believe that the effort toward prevision is important, vast, and unavoidable at the level of the configuration and articulation of materials, as well as relevant for establishing the idea of action according to a productive perspective. However, I also consider it an insufficient basis for the constitution of the architectural object. Preoccupations about prevision, which have in their own way pervaded the course of project-making, must ultimately disappear into the architectural object.

This disappearance is crucial to the constitution of the object itself. It allows the materials ordered by the project to take the form of architecture, and represents the plane of projection between varying conjectures about the future, although it never equals the sum of these projections.

The distance between configuration and constitution is not bridged by deduction or sudden overturnings; on the contrary, it allows the project to weave itself into time, to be slowly and patiently constructed, until its parts and hierarchies become integral and necessary.

Thus prevision, having become a physical, architectural object, transforms itself into prediction, authoritative and solemn, attracting the path of the future toward its own hypothesis, as well as influencing that future's movements.

Architectural prediction starts from a kind of arrest, a kind of hypostatization of the temporal process. It is prediction in that it introduces a clearly demonstrable and atemporal tension into prevision.

Architecture, therefore, displays the characteristics of a figure that is organized by means of a project. This project applies a series of previsions that tend toward an aim and a conclusion, but that must also stand at a distance from that conclusion in order to pre-speak what cannot be said today in any other way.

The conservative point of view seems to resurface here, taking the form of an apparent need for a deductive leap regarding empirical conditions and the way they produce the decisive act of architectural results. This attitude becomes conservative because within it an empty space emerges between the question and the instrument of art, a space that seems regulated only by the subjectivity that sums up and ineffably refracts the things of the world. For architecture, however, that space always represents a separation from some condition. It is produced from the dual concrete material of a limited and specific site and goal, and even seems to make limitation and its description into a structural question regarding the possibility of its own constitution.

THE NECESSARY LIMIT

But if it is true that the question of the project as both production and projection must take specific conditions as the starting point, then architectural prediction becomes concrete on the basis of the criteria by which it defines a situation. The project expands from a point within itself, until it again reaches the hard boundaries of the problem, which may be either close or very distant, and which will have not only spatial but also historical, technical, and political characteristics.

But with the problem of boundaries, we also confront the issue of avoiding imprisonment within their definitions. The issue mainly involves leaving aside the kind of deductive illusions created by those who believe that the project can be guided by a single reading, profound as it may be, of the conditions and context under consideration.

But if it is the architectural interpretation of a situation that introduces and shifts the balance of what exists, that establishes the minimum necessary departure from contextual conditions, and that through this departure grounds the establishment of the space that can be occupied by a specific architectural quality, what then guides the architectural interpretation that allows this departure?

One cannot fail to notice the circularity of this situation, but at the same time it is clearly one of the few dry places in the marsh: a foundation point that is admittedly empirical, but possible, and in that sense necessary.

Modification, belonging, context, identity, specificity, are all words that seem to assume a preexisting reality that should be preserved even while being transformed, that should hand down its memory through traces which themselves are built on earlier evidence. In other words, this reality takes the physical form of a geography whose cult of knowledge and whose interpretation provide the material to support the project.

Despite all attempts to resort to structural interpretations of this material, and thus to histories and symbols that form essences and reasons, it shows itself to be invincibly weak in terms of establishing a project goal that is permeated with a perspective on contingency. At the same time, one necessarily resorts to circumscribing a specific field, and to project-related actions that represent minimal acceptance of generalizations, actions that enumerate and classify only those limited and concrete things contained within the field. But those things are also the symmetrical correspondents of all that remains outside, a measure of the distance and the relationships that are in fact reestablished by each action within the field.

The project as modification of the context places a renewed importance on the historical depth of the present, which is represented in the specific situation. But this often says too little about the direction of the modification, implying that it can be easily deduced from what exists, or that the project will have little trouble extracting the most structurally relevant questions, and thus the main hypotheses that derive from them.

Thus, the proceeding takes on the precarious and conservative form of a new naturalism, whose balance can be upset at any moment by the bursting in of new, unpredictable factors from a source beyond the contextual field under consideration, an interruption that may impatiently upset the order that had been reestablished through patient fieldwork.

But if the invitation to treat the project as a discourse with what exists is motivated also by a wish to cool down, to let settle, to calm the seeming speed of changing opinions and the resulting redundancy of images by drawing on the potential for resistance contained in the positive inertia of what exists, then it is important to ask ourselves whether a project, thus conceived, is truly capable of transforming the conservative tendency that also emerges from this sentiment.

It is possible that, under present conditions, the project of architecture can only present itself as a process of high maintenance and that the new modernity's project of modification can thus describe only that process. Perhaps, today, we need to gather the scattered fragments of our present and clumsily construct with them our "new churches," as was done in the fifth century, which used fragments of ancient architecture as a construction material that was partly gifted with a discourse, whose existence and importance could be felt intuitively but whose meanings remained unknown, and which was laboriously employed as a material for hypotheses with alternate meanings.

This is not a matter of proposing a new collagelike eclecticism (which, in any case, has already been operating for some time), but of thinking about restitching, repairing, reconstructing, and revealing what exists as a possible quality and content for a new architecture.

Even that which places itself in the ostensible vacancy of the landscape, among the miseries of urban peripheries, as well as that which presents itself as the founding act of a settlement, can be governed by the essence of what exists; that is, of what we consider to be durable.

Here we need to speak not about the *apex mentis* of the creative process but about the extremely important work that precedes it: choosing, arranging, sowing, digging, scrutinizing, without presuming to capture the whole experience through the project.

For the time being, it is important to gather and classify the debris of what exists, to make it uniformly archaeological, to reconstruct the reasons for its detached and incomplete form as the foundation of any transformation.

In the architectural project, the current issue is not to create a point from which to observe and describe reality, but rather to illuminate the terrain of reciprocal involvement, and to simultaneously choose the level of reality that can be transformed into architectural substance, in the same way that cartography represents not the whole of reality but that part of reality that can be transformed into a geographical description.

We must therefore think of the new architecture as an architecture of expectation, resistance, and interrogation, modest and firm, a conscious prisoner of the previously mentioned process of high maintenance, which provides guarantees for the new need that forms a part of it. This is the only kind of architecture able to decisively lead toward the autonomy of the project-making process, beyond its own rules of action but also through them.

Such resistance must also be directed against accepting a position of servitude, of functional dependence on popular opinion, which increasingly seems to be forcing architecture to take the form of both escapist decoration and mere instrument.

Today we hear frequent discussions of the gradual differentiation and the increasing complexity of the activities that assume the name of architecture: territorial and urban planning, building construction, engineering, project design, graphics, restoration, classification of environmental resources. They also consider the direct integration of distribution and the market into cycles of production, as well as the history and critique of these different professions. It is unclear whether this represents a voluntary explosion or an authentic need to respond to the proliferation and specialization of activities relating to the project. What is certain is that it raises serious questions about the unity of the discipline and the forms in which it presents itself. This is joined by an ever-increasing complexity within project cycles, driven by a convergence of techniques that include pre-vision, control, and management of the entire system.

On the one hand, all this is undoubtedly related to an enrichment of the territory and materials of our discipline, to the program that William Morris laid out for architecture more than a century and a half ago: that of giving morphological sense to each act whose consequences lead to spatial transformation of the physical environment. But it also relates to ever-tightening limits on the discipline's zone of structural endeavor, to a marginalizing restriction of the discipline to the field of aesthetics, which then becomes a separate, compensatory space in relation to a social structure where being safe, in its widest meaning, has become a fundamental value, or even an obsession. In other words, this process moves toward yet another version of conservatism.

Advanced Mediocrity

The social background that favors the development of an obsession with safety as an aspect of conservation has been aptly defined by Hans Magnus Enzenberger as a condition of "advanced mediocrity." This is a highly defined mediocrity, he says, one that expresses "class conflict as practiced by the middle class and by culture to fill spare time"—a culture that comes to resemble a sort of pedestrian zone. "All this," he continues, "is certainly a success: many nightmares have ended but so have some fundamental conditions for creating works of art."[9]

In architecture, where social conditions have more influence over the product than technical and productive ones, an overbearing diffusion of this different version of conservatism is quite obvious, particularly in the articulation of demands and the ideological assurance that governs them. It suffices to mention the new fundamentalist ideas within various lines of ecological thought (as opposed to legitimate stands against a world of disorder and robbery) and the conditions being dictated by the ambiguous concept of quality of life—or, more specifically, quality of the "natural" environment—all of which represent defense and resistance to change. It is true that in ninety percent of such cases the issue involves not change but deterioration. Still, the blind worship of a known reality as the only arrangement worthy of being either reconstituted or altered in an innocently decorative manner leads to a defensiveness bordering on the kind of historicist positivism that considers all that exists to be valuable simply because it exists. Stylistic reconstruction and *anastylosis,* or their mimeses, are used not as pedagogical tools but rather as valid modes of project-making.

One consequence of this is the transformation of the concept of monument from significant testimony to "cultural asset"—that is, something to be preserved so that it can be spent.

In some cases, the cultural resource even becomes the foundation for planning: sometimes to erase the mistakes (real or supposed) of modernity; at other times, more positively, as a gathering point for structuring a plan around historical and traditional values. This position has all the merits of indisputability that are accorded to any defense of existing values, as well as the limits of conservative good faith.

That progress in architecture sometimes coincides with conservation is, today, probably an inevitable contradiction, but certainly not one without meaning. Nor is it insignificant that institutional apparatuses—when not involved in purely profit-oriented operations—find space for agreement on this terrain, and themselves propose it as a condition for a project.

In the specific practice of composition and its figurative references, there is a clear return to the concept of traditional and finite perspective space, space that is nonetheless full of internal differences and debris, and these differences exhibit the way that space itself is partly shaped by the organization of the project.

The idea of abstraction is dismissed in favor of representation, and of its accompanying tools of drawing, figuration, and professional skill, as well as its measure of narration: nostalgia and memory become preeminent materials. Decoration and ornamental design become subjects of experiment, mainly for their evocative character but also as instruments of figurative mediation between great and small scales, and between building and context, as a form replacing chiaroscuro.

Falsification and noncoincidence seem to acquire not only a renewed legitimacy but also an ability to use unpublished materials. One avoids describing something as it is, substituting instead expressions that refer to what it suggests, in overly literary fashion. Marble appears much more precious when it is imitation marble, because it represents the skill of the craftsman who painted it, the grandeur of the past, an authentic luxury that is not immediately acquirable on the open market. All this also becomes an expression of the sophistication of the project-maker and symbolizes the adoption of an antiegalitarian culture, diversified by groups, where pluralism stems more from tolerant complicity than from a thirst for freedom.

AGAINST VULGAR PLURALISM

It should be said that in the present confusion of varying approaches to architecture, the word "pluralism" seems to have assumed a special legitimating role that appears liberating but actually preserves the status of convictions that are too uniformly shared. In the name of complete openness, or of indifference (it is unclear which), pluralism is invoked as a defense against the threats of rigidity and ideological intolerance, and thus simultaneously fosters the present configuration of society, along with the minor chaos and great void that surround it.

But misinterpreted pluralism also transforms casual choices, mere subjective assertions, into false certainties; rather than constructing freedom, it allows repose. It does not eliminate ideology, but only transforms it into an ideology of common sense, of "they say," of "it must seem this way," and even of "it obviously appears this way."

Moreover, this interpretation of pluralism transforms transgressive efforts into mere self-confirmation, into exorcising the obstacle of radical and specific ideas. For all to be different, that is, all different within the same inefficient mode of forming values, seems to be the most direct result of all this.

We are infinitely grateful to pluralism for preventing massacres and coercion, but pluralism also infinitely expands the reasonable, secure indifference of the empire of apparatuses and astute behavior.

The possibility of expressing an opinion obviously guarantees nothing about its quality; it is a condition that permits, not a horizon that constructs. Moreover, all possibilities need not necessarily be put into practice. On the contrary, the polycentricity of opportunities should accentuate a trend toward responsibility, driven by a hypothetical and ethical desire. Uncertainty ought to increase the ethical weight of choice, but this happens only rarely.

The social advantages of pluralism weaken the obsessive and positive convictions that are indispensable to creative research in artistic practice. In our specific discipline, this brings to the forefront a type of architect that lacks the necessary tensions, an architect without means of travel, with eyes full of dust, whose behavior is determined, and whose work is conditioned, by fear of constructing a position as well as by anxieties about being up-to-date.

In recent decades, praise for the idea of pluralism, and for the values of peaceful coexistence and democratic ethics that are supposed to come with it, has been given a growing emphasis. But although its principles are fundamental to human coexistence, and might be interpreted in the direction of a rational ethic, it remains unclear whether pluralism offers any positive contribution to transforming the dynamics of artistic practice.

How, from a pluralistic standpoint, does one form and legitimize a judgment of quality in architecture, the kind of judgment that divides, accuses, and defends its positions and intentional results?

Does this judgment consider consistency between internal principles and results, thus becoming a strictly internal assessment, or is it the kind of aesthetic judgment that has been a matter of infinite opinion ever since it became a variable independent of principles and horizons? Is it a judgment of ability in terms of talent and professionalism, an ability that serves a variety of positions? Is it a judgment regarding "harmony and invention," which today means conformity to the invasion of fashion and the contrivance of the day? Is it a judgment of flexibility or firmness, of availability or precision, for the short term or the long?

Not even the principle of mastering construction techniques seems to be a firm point any more, since for some time now architects seem to have abdicated this responsibility in favor of the project as a finished product. This abdication occurs even though the technical quality of the building depends largely on the conditions of the market and the state of advancement of production, rather than on the quality of the project. Even the efficiency of a building's realization seems to lie completely in the efficiency of management and the political opportunity of the architecture-product.

But is this really a condition of pluralism, or is it one where fragments of great ideas that exploded some years ago float in the vast, oily liquid of the management of mass culture? Is this really pluralism—that is, a debate among different principles, ideas, and perspectives—or is it a condition of infinite reinterpretation (which, as we have seen, many consider positive), where not only do the different positions move in continuous reciprocal oscillation, but every principle transforms its own nature indifferently and continuously.

One way or the other, it is clear that the suspension of dialectical reflection we are experiencing profoundly contradicts the pull toward materiality, duration, and stability on which the tradition of our discipline is built. How (and whether) to prevent this tradition from becoming a mere decoration of the "society of spectacle" (a decoration that has now taken on the name of "design," which in common language means the interpretation of fashion rather than a tradition of method) is an important task, to be carried out without defensiveness or evasion.

We certainly cannot take seriously childish attempts to express the great value of pluralism through the neoformalism of transience and interruption, a true caricature of liberty. Nor can we conceive of architecture as a calligraphy exercise of the avant-garde, or even less turn our eyes toward a consoling and nonrepeatable past.

On the other hand, the paths that return to a rigorous functionality of technique and economy are also precluded, because technique and economy have, pluralistically, become functions of the market, of management, and of the organization of money. They have thrown aside their firm and consistent objectivity, and adopted the variably interpretable notions of investment, image, rebalancing, and global bartering.

Functionality and technique have lost most of their character as mimeses of a rationality that places social and moral rationality before productive rationality; they, too, have adopted the law of opportunity.

The previously mentioned appeal to context, to land, and to their history can instead be read as an attempt to use the opportunities of pluralism in proper and specific fashion, in order to repropose points of reference capable of discontinuous, long-lasting resistance: essentially, an attempt to escape from the intangibility of vulgar pluralism.

This is the present challenge: to oppose vulgar pluralism by building, from the ground and from the site, a new imagination capable of giving essential meaning to the light emitted by the concept of prediction, whose features I attempted earlier to define. But when prediction and antiquity, site and ground, seem to join together in this effort of resistance, in a nostalgic yearning for ideological certainty, then everything becomes approximate, dulled, wrapped in itself, and can make only an illusory (that is, a conservative) appeal to the good old days when artistic practice was in apparent solidarity with a specific social condition. Thus, in the absence of trust in one's own expressive means, one wishes to reappropriate all possible others (as I am likewise doing here), or to return instead, against all *techne*, to a kind of discipline that is wholly autonomous and, in turn, completely illusory. From a certain point of view, a contradictory symmetry thus arises within the conservative attitude: on one hand, a dissemination of purposely ineffable meanings; on the other, a desire for rules of action and judgment that takes the form of an appeal to the strength of tradition.

But conservatism, like all appeals to tradition and all nostalgic yearnings, also forms an aspect of the triumphant culture of escape, of that culture that exists only because it falls short of its own objective, that of looking ahead in order to build a fragment of truth. As Aldo Gargani wrote some time ago,

> The fault of contemporary culture is that, in its project, it is essentially a culture of escape. . . . If the form allows itself to be seen; if upon encountering a new building we find nothing for us, but rather the projective identification of the architect, this is a symptom of a culture of architecture that is a culture of escape.[10]

Whether this culture represents the ideological incarnation of today's dominating majority class is yet another matter, not without consequence, but perhaps for the moment without alternatives.

An advantage to be drawn from this difficult situation may involve the reconstitution of a necessary minority—not the frivolous minority of fashion, nor the obligatory one of poverty, but a minority of choice and of patient discipline.

Such a minority would have none of the glorious characteristics of the great avant-gardes of the past. It would occupy the opposite pole with respect to the phenomenon of reabsorption of neo-avant-gardes, however disguised, by the "homogeneous society"—a felicitous reabsorption that has been conspicuously active for more than twenty years. It would be a patient minority, one able to consider duration without conceit, monuments without monumentalism; a minority capable of deep respect for skills and techniques, without the ideology of a craftsman's leather apron, and without any naive faith in the powers of hypermodern technological society; a minority able to take pleasure in free invention as the necessary solution to a question, not as frivolity. A minority whose acts would respect an economy of expressive means, as well as a simplicity achieved by passing through the complexities of reality without oversimplifying them; a minority capable of continuously constructing a critical distance from reality, above all from an overjustified context; a minority capable of rebuilding within itself the diversity required in a quest for clarity, but without undue pride over the momentary certainties that this produces; a minority that wishes to remain outside of fashion and of image; a minority capable of returning materiality to the embodiment of things.

This minority would of course be in a continually precarious balance, its points of support in danger of being misinterpreted or reversed in meaning. It would be more certain of its own denials than its assertions, and would constantly challenge the commitments of fundamentalists, the fatalism of historicists, and above all those who speak of art with too little modesty.

Definition, measure, integrity of form and construction, identification of the relationship between space and manufactured work, between manufactured work and the land, would be the main instruments in the architecture of this minority.

I admit that this is probably a rather naive portrait, one motivated by those most dangerous of advisers, moral outrage and good intention. It is naive because it is based on the desire for an authentically rational reorganization of the present, something that no one has called for, and also naive in its own nostalgia for the project.

"Let it be," goes a song that has influenced my generation in the past quarter of a century. But to let anything be is, today, no simple or natural matter; it requires the difficult reconquest of a state of readiness that is not at all blind to the contradictions of the world. It is an invitation to become, but not, therefore, to stop being.

PART TWO: WAYS AND INSTRUMENTS

On Precision

In his famous essay "From the World of Approximation to the Universe of Precision," published in *Critique* in 1948, Alexandre Koyré wrote about how the application of mathematics to the physical world—that is, the very nature of "physics"—seemed paradoxical to the ancient world:

> Greek thought remained obstinately faithful to such ideas, whichever philosophies they were deduced from, and never admitted that exactness might belong to this world, that the matter of this world, of our own world, of the sublunar world might embody mathematical beings, except when forced by art. Indeed, there is nothing more precise than the design of a base or a capital, or the shape of a Greek column: nothing is better calculated—nor with more refinement—than their respective measurements. But it is art that imposes them on nature.[11]

But while art in the ancient world was considered the activity that could produce precision, even precision as perfection, it seems that art takes on a new role in today's society, attempting to exist outside measure-taking scientific and technological thought. It does this either by describing the latter's conditions and limits, or through repeated attempts to present truths and facts that lie outside areas of scientific control. Somehow, it seems that the main task of art is precisely to produce things that defy measurement, or that raise, also from an epistemological point of view, the need to find instruments of measure based not on the constancy of structures, but rather on the nature of the ever-changing constellation of relationships that connects them.

Obviously, not everyone agrees with such a definition of this preeminent feature of modern creative production: and they are not without reason.

Indeed, one should not forget that within the modern tradition the rules of precision (as a mimesis of the methods and objectives of science) have dominated the principles of art in general and architecture in particular, to the point of turning architecture into a champion of nihilism in the very age of science and technique. This comes not only through a mimesis of the machine, with its mechanical precision and rhythms, but also through the very idea of self-reference, and thus the idea that the instruments specific to a discipline form the first issue that must be engaged in order to make works of art: the specifics of film and music production; the idea of "truth in painting" as a reduction to the meaningful application of colors on a flat surface; and so on. All this is therefore not only the main rule of modern creative action, but also a special interpretation of that rule that becomes above all a narrative of the *technē* itself.

The concept of function (borrowed from mathematics as well as biology), and thus the principle of the constituting form as related to the search for the essence of the problem under consideration, also characterizes an effort toward precision as objectivity, as production and nonreproduction of new realities. In fact, through its essential nondescriptiveness, a discussion of precision's own constitutional processes becomes the focus of creative labor. In the form of *epistēmē*, precision as a model of thought has directly influenced (this is an obvious thing to say) the tradition of modern art. Today it has even assumed the particular configuration of invisible precision. This occurs when it no longer takes the form of utensils, machines, or manufactured articles, but rather becomes a purely ideal process, pure bodiless function, as well as when it presents itself as mimesis and proof of the exactness of previsions and their calculation.

Symbols of this in architecture include, for example, the idea of the endless divisibility of space, or the use of transparency as a means of expression, or when the facades of a building become a mirror, in which the corporeal substance of architecture disappears and surroundings reflect and measure themselves with the mute precision of specularity.

Naturally, in Alexandre Koyré's argument, the word "precision" always means the ability to measure exactly, depending on conceptual rules and necessities. Within his argument, he leaves aside other meanings such as that of "precise" as rigorously respectful of orders and rules, or again that of *praecisus,* stripped of all superfluous elements, or "precise" as corresponding to an exact meaning—interpretations that are highly relevant to the practice of architecture.

To architects, precision can have three different, though interconnected, meanings. It can mean that each work constructs its own set of rules, which establish their own specific order for changing what exists as well as the discipline's traditions. It can also mean that every part of an organized act within the work must be completely consistent with those specific rules. Finally, it can mean that the work must be built with maximum technical and expressive economy regarding its own needs, that such means must therefore converge without waste in every element of the work, and that the acuteness of such means is proportional to their transformative ability.

Precise also means being able to suspend judgment on ideologies and historical periods; to create space and silence around reflections on the project; to listen lucidly to its internal voices; and to define and resolve its knots and problems, arranging things in mutual relationships that tend toward a recovery of the original act of joining together in pursuit of a goal.

Precision also means a clear, firm image that resists the proliferation of market images which, devoid of internal needs, dissolve one into the other, leaving a strong sense of extraneousness and unease. Precision means the ability to describe nuances with exactitude; an ability to see through things with subtlety, to know and weigh the value of a detail, to understand the significance of absences, of pauses, of emptiness, of variation, and of the relationship between architectural objects as well as their individual forms.

Precision means that every piece of the project, however small, must be entirely legible, revealing not its own independence but the necessity behind both its existence and its connections with other elements, as well as the reasons why each of those elements was selected.

The reasons for these choices must, in turn, be intelligible when they are offered as a deliberate turn away from consistency in a project, so that each solution shows itself to be the only point of balance within the labyrinth of possible solutions.

And as project organization becomes more precise it also becomes more flexible (in a positive sense). In other words, it becomes capable of facing and describing complex conditions, as well as minute oscillations between different horizons of meaning.

Precision is not a synonym for rigidity; instead, it is the instrument necessary for exploring and establishing the limits of ambiguity in a project. Only a remarkably precise expression can become a plane of reference for varying meanings, raise varying interpretations, and therefore create a different collective meaning for the architectural work.

Precise is that which enlightens, whose intention is to clarify: thus, it is that which moves away from obscurity, from contradiction—not to erase, hide, or resolve it, but to reveal all its possible richness of interpretation. Exactly because the description of confusion differs from a confused description, only maximum precision makes it possible to speak about ambiguity, suspensions, voids, stratifications of meanings.

Precision is light of touch and able to work strategic modifications on discrete points, as well as in vast spaces. It always presents itself as a mysterious image that reveals the logic of its construction only gradually, and after long and careful observation.

Precise also means neat, without smears, uncertain residuals, or patchwork: it means punctually clarified, inimitable in the way it is made. A precise architecture may be exactly reproduced as a manufactured object, but it is at the same time absolutely unique in its response to the meaning of its goal, its site, and its specific historical condition.

Finally, precise means limited, chosen, and defined.

Today it is no longer possible to think of a totality that is anything but potential, conjectural, multiple; only a taste for mental order, precision, and transparent intelligence is capable of gathering and communicating this totality. This seems possible by first ascertaining the conditions for an intervention—its physical context, its aim, and the state of the discipline—then gauging how deep one must dig to make a secure foundation, and finally by choosing the indispensable materials of construction and defining the method required to unveil the truth of the specific situation: that is, the essence of its real content. Through precision one learns with patient repetition to construct the fabric of a project whose organizing weft contains structure, color, design, matter, and form.

An elucidation of a specific project's meaning must also be limited, chosen, and defined. It is not important that other ideas and future eras may lend it different content and meaning.

Naturally, the question of precisely defining the limits of an individual case, and of its truth, also raises the problem of avoiding imprisonment within this definition; that is, the problem of evading duplication, of seeing the project as mere completion, continuity, and extension.

Precision must thus never present itself as a tautology. Rather, it is an instrument of penetration and unveiling, and thus of the establishment of difference.

The effort toward precision is also the ethical form of the work, the imperative that leads from indistinct but acute sensations to their equally acute expression. Precision becomes the foundation for the very morality of the creative work. It strives to be that which pushes one to clarify, to establish, and to describe emotion as precisely as possible; that is, in depth.

We know well that this "precise description" of memories and wishes is actually "precise construction," modification, and movement. In fact, it is the apparent impossibility of an absolutely complete and persuasive expression that launches a movement toward precision, the constitution of the work of architecture.

It is obvious that every art has its own specific system of norms, which vary over time and which regulate its practical and instrumental realization. Less obvious is the answer to a question discussed innumerable times: what, if any, is the organizational influence of technique upon a specific work of art? In other words, how important is professional skill and its specific use for a defined aim; but also how much does it matter that technique is a means toward something else, and at the same time carries the significance of its own history as an instrument? And finally, what place does the question of technique (by no means a technical problem) occupy in the process of forming a work? Naturally, all this began when distinctions were drawn between practical and conceptual action, between heights of ability and depths of reflection, which in the ancient world were united in the concept of *technē.*

If, for the moment, we put aside everything that technical and techno-scientific thought has altered in the area of project technique as an autonomous product (and it is a lot), then technique presents itself as material for the architectural project on two different levels. On one level, techno-scientific thought and industrial production have gradually established themselves as an increasingly prominent and direct component of architecture during the past century. This component became an expressive model and instrument of radical renewal in the age of hope, when technical reproducibility was considered a way for art to imagine a free, equal, and progressive society. The age of integration has, instead, adopted a model of truth and expression of power-wishes aptly described by Max Bense when he says that art and science in the age of technology are always the art and science of technology.[12] This does not exclude the possibility that what we have until now considered to be architecture and its tradition may be completely incompatible with the techno-scientific world, or indeed that the latter may already have decided to proceed without what we consider to be architecture.

This influence of the idea of technique upon architecture does not, however, invalidate all that work that refuses to join peacefully with the techno-scientific idea. On the contrary, I am convinced that the best architectures of our century are born under the sign of the contradictions involved in this alignment, of critique for this alignment and even radical opposition to it; but this still remains our fixed point of reference.

The second level comprises specific construction techniques, with their traditions and dynamics. Construction technique in fact involves the organization of a set of techniques at different levels of development, techniques that are often separately elaborated and that are arranged according to a unitary aim defined specifically by the project. The methods for joining different parts of the construction system thus become the elements requiring the most effort, and are often the points at which the application of specific inventions becomes most critical. In one sense, these methods form the technique of architectural construction. But one must admit that the organic unity of the techniques used to build Gothic cathedrals was incomparably higher, more refined, consistent, and technologically significant than the construction modes we confront today. Gothic architects transformed materials into architectural facts; we assemble products.

Naturally, techniques of assemblage can themselves become techniques of composition, and it is possible that semi-refined products may, in the future, take on the natural archaeological quality of antique construction materials. However, since production no longer means giving form to materials, but instead involves arranging products, we should always keep in mind that different construction-related activities by nature bring together premanufactured materials, endowed with separate meanings that generally originate not from the experience of construction but rather from the rules of production and market competition for each product.

But while the production of manufactured goods proceeds through successive refinements of the same genre of product, building construction (apart from the accumulation of general experiences) is each time a *unicum* expressed through a unique field condition and a particular objective, and on a site whose circumstances are only weakly transferable.

Thus, each architectural work annexes particular alignments that are open to experimental risks; in one sense, each constructs not only a language but also a specific technique. One might therefore say that the only language common to techniques of building construction is an accepted system of representation used in projects for the realization of specific works. Each project must confront the difficulty of giving unique architectural unity to cultures that differ not only technically but also in their specific objectives and modes of representation.

But among the activities most strongly connected with the use of techniques, building construction is one of the slowest and least sensitive in assimilating technical evolutions (except perhaps in its mimesis of the idea of technique). It is particularly slow to acquire experiences from the technologies and materials in other fields of manufacture.

Climate control in an automobile is technically resolved through physical measurements and tolerances that no construction product can attain today. Experiences in the aeronautical field have yielded a series of technologies regarding the joining of materials that building construction has only begun to consider. This is also true for tool miniaturization, protection from external agents, dynamic wear, and so on.

Moreover, the different production costs offered by competing manufacturers for the same construction product prove the immaturity (especially in Italy) of this type of industry, which for years has pursued a rather ideological attempt to rationalize production largely through prefabrication, or which has built its profits on real estate speculation rather than building. Although the relationship between project and execution certainly remains one of the weak points of the system, one should not think to resolve this discontinuity by allowing the construction industry to absorb the project. This would inevitably mean the end of any possibilities of dialectic in project-making.

On the other hand, the attention that is from time to time devoted to particular technical aspects (integration of different building projects, of scales of intervention, of project and product maintenance; but also energy conservation, the "intelligent building," internal pollution, etc.) has often, up to now, had more to do with ideology than with any meaningful contribution to the field of architecture.

It remains true, in any case, that techniques appear in the construction of an architectural project in three main ways: (1) as tectonics, the skeleton of a building, the substantial structure of the manufactured object (some even say that the structure of architecture is the architecture of its structure); (2) as physiology, in terms of supply, of flows of services that can be controlled and activated (this view is becoming highly decisive, in part because of the way it has influenced form); and finally (3) as an exercise of detail.

Obviously, such a distinction between these three aspects and those that preside over the form, measurement, distribution, and spatial definition of the architectural organism and its contextual relationships (techniques that in some ways have assumed a more important role in the discipline's recent tradition) is used only to develop the argument. In reality, the project of architecture consists precisely in the meaningful organization of all these different techniques through their reciprocal use within the work.

Naturally, this does not have to mean reducing the tasks of the project to a mere organization of their compatibilities. We at least have the responsibility to reconnect techniques to a place and an aim, through a form that should always reconstitute the meaning of the subject under consideration and at the same time represent the only possible form of architectural existence for that specific arrangement of techniques.

But undoubtedly such aspects are, so to speak, placed at varying distances from the center of the project, and a change in their reciprocal hierarchies becomes an element in defining the project's identity, rather than simply an instrument to realize an architectural vision of the world that precedes the material essence of the specific object.

If anything, the science of separate processes of control (for example the structure versus other aspects of construction) has distanced rather than integrated the nature of building with respect to the center of the project. This has occurred not only because those processes have been removed from the specific abilities of the discipline, but also because their advancement has made it possible to consider almost every typology of their use independently. This causes their contribution to the definition of the architectural object to oscillate from domination to complete marginality, and thus reduces their influence.

On the other hand, the strategy of detail is certainly among the technical elements most critical to our discipline, and one that marks change in the language of architecture. It is therefore important to constantly examine the ways that architectural details are formed, and to emphasize that, according to the famous saying of Auguste Perret, "Il n'y a pas de détail dans la construction," that is, detail is not merely a detail.[13]

For example, all the reasons explained above show the great error in the belief that development of details can be entrusted to cultures such as those of industry and construction. This might be convenient and economical for the project-maker, but it leads toward an unprecedented decay in architecture.

Clearly, detail does not depend mechanically on any overall concept, although it must have structural relations to such a concept. Detail does not exist solely to declare general decisions; rather, it gives direct form to such decisions, embodies their physical existence, and renders the meaning of different parts articulate and recognizable.

An illusion frequently arises that on one hand it is enough to replace detail with quotation, as an element that enters architectural language already endowed with meaning, and on the other, that a grand overall concept can dominate and automatically permeate all aspects of a project, including its details. In built architecture, the result is often either a strong feeling of arbitrariness, of superimposed ornamentality, or a disagreeable feeling of oversimplification, of an enlarged model, of a lack of articulation in its parts at different scales: walls like cut-out cartons, windows like unfinished, empty holes, and on the whole, a sharp decline in tension between the drawing and the constructed building.

For example, one can observe how the eloquent detail of the fifties, which focused on analyzing and making explicit the material furnished by the principles of composition of the architectural object, was followed by a phase of reduced expression in which architectural detail was reabsorbed into the overall concept of a building.

At its best, this absorption involved not elimination, but rather a different way of thinking about the hierarchy relating detail to the whole, a way of creating implicit connections between planes, relationships between materials, and differences in the figurative use of parts.

This takes on a double meaning. On the one hand, it means distancing oneself from the value of constructive and tectonic truth as a supporting idea for the formation of the architectural figure. On the other, it means questioning the ability of detail to represent itself as a cell of the whole. The eloquent aphasia that results from either case has been precipitously occupied by a revival of decoration, or rather by ornamentation in the form of stylistic quotation, often as an infraction of a fundamental rule of contemporary architecture, the methodological rule of the organic.

It seems that in the past few years, critics and historians alike have been doing their utmost to demonstrate the legitimacy, indeed the indispensability, of ornament in the construction of a work of art. We can even say that they busied themselves trying to demonstrate the illegitimacy of the systematic exclusion of ornament from modern art, and especially from the architecture of the modern movement.

Thanks to its notion of successive embellishment, even though it is organic, the word "ornament" is probably more suitable than "decoration," which is somehow more strongly related to elements of the classical and historical language of architecture, and is often used in treatises to refer to the concept of expression.

If we put aside the naive interpretation of functionalism as univocal correspondence between the form and solution of practical problems (of technique, distribution, comfort, etc.), and consider an architectural project as a process that reveals the essence of a specific phenomenon, dense with all its debris and contradictions, then the programmatic absence of ornament in the practice of contemporary architecture will seem better grounded and understandable, and the suspicion that modernity feels toward the decorative, particularly the kind of decoration that is expressed in a mimesis of modern architectural language, will also seem more justified. From this point of view, it is useless to discuss whether the characteristics of the discipline consist of its style of language and ornament or of its principles of use and construction, because the problem of architecture is precisely the meaningful organization of all such issues.

I am reminded of the famous exchange between Picasso and Braque on the subject of how a nail is produced, whether from iron or from the idea of a nail. The effort of the modern project has been to understand that the idea of a nail inextricably participates in the nail's physical being, and in the refoundation of its instruments and objectives, and that invention thus lies not only in the form of the nail, or only in its material, but in rethinking the essence of its aim in a specific circumstance.

The problem of contemporary artistic practice is not sublimation but truth: to show things as they are, to bring as much clarity as possible into their competing relationships in order to provoke other relationships that may be ancient, or new, or simply richer and wider.

If this is the crucial, necessary issue that directs and organizes all materials, and formulates hypotheses around itself, then the question of ornamentation must be incorporated in the project from the very start, rather than serving as the mode by which "problems of engineering" enter the world of aesthetics.

Ornamentation can therefore emerge within the process of forming a project not only as a style but also as a complex notion of space, a strategy for an articulate use of materials, a mediation between the form and materiality of the building through the exercise of detail, a process establishing the hierarchy of different parts, a heightened complexity in the relationships between interior and exterior, light and shadow, and so on.

Apart from some rather pathetic attempts to resort directly to ornamentation in the styles of the past (which is probably a naive way to use the principle of mimesis to answer the serious questions of symbolism and relationship with context), the heightened complexity obtained, in general, by the superimposition of languages, the fragmentation of parties, and the brusque emphasis on inconsistencies between interior and exterior, use and space, construction and expression—that is, the new incarnations of ornamentation—can, despite the coarseness of their results, be considered signs of a trend toward forms of architectural narration, to use a widely metaphorical term.

This question might, of course, also be considered from a more pessimistic point of view, by noting on the one hand the gradual slippage of architecture toward a concept of itself as a scenographic social activity, a mere instrument of mercantile promotion; and on the other, the survival of architecture as one of many signs that opposes the formation of any specific imagination.

In short, one might say that architecture no longer needs decoration, because it has itself become nothing but a transitory decoration of mass society.

Since I am neither pessimistic nor resigned, I firmly believe that architecture has other tasks. Certainly, if architecture can increasingly see itself as a necessary endeavor, then a renewed discussion of ornament and decoration will be possible.

On Monumentality

I believe that no distinction can be made between the architectural monument and the specific morphological quality of architecture. For one who builds or designs projects, the wish to create duration and collective meaning over time (in other words, the reason behind making monuments) is closely connected to the question of quality. In modernity, quality rests on the level of our inquiry into not only our rules of action but also the very meaning of artistic action. This raises numerous contradictions regarding the exclusively affirmative character of what we traditionally consider to be a "monument."

When a monument becomes the content of artistic practice, subject to critical self-questioning, much of its monumental nature is denied, because that nature comes from tradition. From this point of view an unresolved conflict in fact exists between the monument and modernity.

But although modernity often presents itself as programmatically opposed to established beliefs, I do not think that this has anything to do with the inadequacy or inability of modernity to construct the collectively symbolic. Rather it concerns a contradiction within the very notion of monument, and in the monument's present ability to legitimately represent, within any creative practice, the grand historical tradition that we have been helping to demolish for at least a century. In relation to that grand tradition, present-day monuments seem instead to be a form of compensation, of illusory projection, and of nostalgia. In such cases, monuments can only be founded on inherited material, and the only choices involve which handed-down piece should become the reference for one's interpretation.

I say all this also because I consider the modern project to be in no sense the realization of a definitive universality, but rather, as I have said in the first part of this book, a project capable of surpassing itself through critical reason. This kind of reason does not measure itself only by the relationship between needs and means, or define itself solely by its own abilities to perform. Instead, it considers aims, objectives, and principles as necessary hypotheses in relation to instruments, and is able to distinguish between different types of reasons, including the reason of the monument.

As everyone knows by now, the mature historiography of architecture has taught for some time that the modern movement cannot be reduced to a single form, and that diversified, rich, and complex souls have thrived within this movement.

And everyone who adopts a broader perspective toward the general notion of modernity, even when only to announce its demise, often refers to those same complex thinkers, who are fundamental to a definition of modernity as a critical epoch.

Regarding Saint-Simon's famous distinction between organic and critical epochs, it is clear that modernity belongs to the latter; and that in thought as in character, its faith in its ability to proceed necessarily involves proceeding through a crisis toward a solution that is always known to be provisional.

What, indeed, is modernity, and our discipline's adventure within it, if not the ability to see and surpass one's own contradictions through critical reason? What is modernity, if not the ability to use one's own transformative tensions, without illusions but also without cynicism, to enter the world, to understand it, and to participate in it through one's own hypotheses?

The hypotheses of architecture as an artistic practice in the end present themselves as clearly demonstrable facts. Transformative tensions are expressed not through description but by introducing a new architectural object into the world, an object that moves and divides rather than interprets. In this sense, we can speak of the artistic object as a monument. But we must also speak about the difficult conditions of monumental representation with regard to the collective meaning of a work.

Of course, it is still possible (as recent history has amply proved) to build monuments of great quality, with great teaching value, dense with historical memory, that testify to some present project. But this involves entirely special notions of memory and testimony, which transform them into materials that form a horizon as necessary as it is consciously provisional; a horizon endowed with a strong subjective direction.

The monument, when defined as the significant morphological value of a work, is in any case neither a theme nor a typology, nor can it be an explicit objective. One cannot order the construction of a "monument" (in the meaning that I have attempted to define above) in the same way that one orders the construction of a school or theater, even though this is often done, and architects frequently try to pursue this task even when their clients have not requested it. The monument is also not a genre (as for example, the novel is for literature), nor a rhetorical form, nor a category of composition: it is hard to think of it as a creative material that can be as easily invoked as these.

From this point of view, it also becomes difficult to adopt the fashionable attitude of completely dismissing the polemical stance some architects of the modern movement have displayed toward the idea of monument. They were right on at least one point: the monument is not a question of monumentality, and the attempt to establish the effect that a work will have on those who experience it is one of the classic ways to produce kitsch.

We can certainly say that today there seems to be an increasingly insistent wish to represent oneself through monuments (a desire that seems to me abstract, a form of subjective, illusory projection in its identification of the symbols it is supposed to bear). In other words, one wishes to represent oneself beyond the present, or to represent subjectively recognized memories in the present.

This is a longing for permanence, which reacts against uncertainty, against continuous change, and against the value given to the instantaneous, the immaterial, and the temporary. Unfortunately, the antifunctionalism that accompanies this wish often takes the form of aspiration toward literary symbolism and expression, as well as aestheticism in itself, which becomes a consolatory category.

Another present-day response to the widespread desire for monuments, one that is founded on the hierarchies of society and power in more positivistic fashion, is the monument conceived as "corporate image." This is most convincingly proved by the new style of multinational economic power, where a desire for monuments is transformed into a monumental order with all its declamatory character, enacted either as an appeal to the past as a legitimating form, or by turning to the ideal of modernization as stylistic abstraction.

But I believe that we must not confuse "corporate image" with monument, although the self-promotional efforts of institutional powers now imitate the former, which strives to impress an inimitable commercial identity on collective memory, and to see openings in mass behavior as a sign, not a value. It does not construct indicators of meaning or horizons by which to measure oneself; neither does it point out potential examples. Rather, it positivistically affirms its unavoidable existence, and attempts to engrave a name and a performance (before anything concrete) in the unstable memory of the consumer.

However, there is an undeniable relationship between the notion of monument and the past thirty years of discussions inside architecture about the value of memory. If no value is given to the memory of past and present events, then there is no reason to build monuments for their future testimony. Nor would there be any reason to worry about the future existence of the value that we bring into being through the construction of architecture.

But this relationship between memory and monument is in fact somewhat more complicated. The historical avant-garde has built, in apparent polemic against memory, extraordinarily imposing monuments. These impress through their themes and morphological value, as well as by their evident collective significance. This is true whether this significance is seen as non-repeatable and unique or as a notable example that one hopes to reinterpret or repeat.

Walter Gropius, responding to a discussion promoted in 1948 by *The Architectural Review* on the subject of the monument and the tradition of functionalism, consistently declared that he considered a series of territorial transformations by the Tennessee Valley Authority to be a great monument, thus showing how vast and unconventional the modern notion of monument could be.[14]

Indeed, we know that many monuments of antiquity (or at least those we consider monuments) originated as exorcisms rather than admonitions. Today we also consider some extraordinary realizations by ancient engineering to be monuments, from aqueducts to bridges and fortifications, whose intentions at the planning stage were undoubtedly anything but monumental.

Moreover, even objects whose use or meaning we do not know have been elevated to the rank of monument, because of their rarity as evidence, as trace, or because of their very special relationship with the site, which they are able to transform by naming it, or even through restricting access. Here, the monument approaches the idea of the marvelous, the extraordinary, the astonishing. As Marcel Duchamp has taught us, even a common object can become a monument if it is inside a museum, if the marvel springs from a new interpretation of the object within a different context.

Michel Foucault is therefore right when he says that "l'histoire est ce qui transforme les documents en monuments," meaning that collective conscience and intentionality construct the monument by projecting a system of meanings and memories onto a specific object.[15]

As architects, all we can do is construct projects and material objects able to present themselves at such a high level of integrity, tension, subtlety, depth of connection, and invention that they are worthy of becoming, by means of history, monuments.

No new architecture can arise without modifying what already exists, but the interest surrounding the notion of modification in recent years is not based on such an obvious consideration, at least if we view modification as recognizing the importance of what exists as structural material, rather than mere background, during the design process.

The project as modification also tells us that each situation offers a specific truth, to be sought and revealed as the essence of the goal, and as the truth of both the site and the geography that embodies that site's particular history. This raises the question of whether one can transfer project experiences; that is, to what degree not only models but also methods, including the case-by-case method, can be transformed.

I would thus like to suggest that this conception of modification has gradually assumed a special importance as the conceptual instrument that presides over the project of architecture; that despite its widely varying interpretations, it might be considered the most continuous and structural element of the changes that have occurred within the theory of architectural design during the past thirty years.

We could even ask whether it might be possible to describe a language of modification, or a set of languages of modification, just as the years of the avant-garde saw a series of languages of the new.

To that end, we need to begin by considering that in the past thirty years architectural culture has, often in divergent ways and with questionable outcomes, shown a growing interest in another notion that accompanies modification: the notion of belonging. Even within the modern tradition, this notion of belonging (to a tradition, a culture, a place, and so on) opposes the idea of a *tabula rasa,* a new beginning, an isolated object, an infinitely and indifferently divisible space, which distinguishes the constructivist avant-garde. It also clearly opposes the internationalization of the techniques, finance, powers, tastes, and mass behavior that surrounds us, and from which we benefit in the sense that it has allowed the avant-garde concept of space to gain a highly productive techno-economic significance.

But one must also turn to this notion of belonging in order to explain the avant-garde's interest in the materials of memory, not nostalgically but in terms of juxtaposition, collage, *objet trouvé,* of forming new orders and groupings by shifting the context of those materials that belong to memory's heritage.

We might, in essence, ask ourselves how much the great success of the idea of "estrangement," so widespread during the classical period of the avant-garde, owes to the dialectical discourse with its specific context; that is, to what extent the existence of a rule of belonging is essential for this exception.

The efforts of the architectural avant-garde have always been to pursue novelty as a value in itself, fostering special ties with the idea of the manufacturing process, of which architecture becomes a mimesis. But the notion of belonging instead embodies an interest in the continuity found in the history of the discipline, and in the idea of place both as identity and as impure material. The notion of belonging develops transverse relationships for which project design primarily represents a process of modification: one that attracts and organizes the debris contained in the context, and that constructs from those pieces asymmetry, varying density, and the values of diversity.

The history of this transformation is slow, complex, and certainly not rectilinear. It is formed by tensions rather than reconciliations. It belongs to the modern tradition, both to its moderate forms and (when observed with sufficient historical detachment) to the differences that reach beyond individual creative personalities to articulate even the most radical realizations of European rationalism between the two wars, and to render them specific to varying cultural and physical situations.

Differences between sites were already considered as a value in the fifties, through Ernesto N. Rogers's theory of environmental preexistence, and through the interest in history as project material: a history that criticizes and articulates the very idea of a modern movement, expanding its meaning and boundaries and transforming it from a position into a tradition.

With the growing interest in the city and the territory as preeminent materials for both the subject and the content of the architectural project, the idea of belonging truly becomes a pedagogy for the project.

Urban analysis, which involves the study of cities and of the relationship between morphology and typology, as well as the principles of settlement, environment, and geography as history, has laid the groundwork for an increasingly defined interest in place as a foundation for the project.

Regarding the theme of specific context, the project has access to two methods. In one, the answer is mimetic, stylistic, seeking conciliation, taking up motifs and symbols. The other produces neither conciliation nor apparent assimilation but rather juxtaposition; within it the transformation of relationships itself takes on the value of a language, or a tendency to form languages. If we aspire to employ the kind of quality that stems from commitment to the specific situation as the essence of the particular aim and the truth of the site, then not only do differences become values, but project-making comes to mean modifying the very rules of our belonging.

This seems to overturn the famous Beaux-Arts debate between *parti* as model and *rendu* as expression, in which the latter, as the interpretation of the specific situation, becomes the structure for establishing the former.

The techniques used by the project derive from the profession's rules and the discipline's tradition, but the project becomes concrete through its clash with the site and the specific situation.

For the rest, the project must recognize the present impossibility of any natural coincidence with the site. The quality of architecture lies above all in the quality of that noncoincidence. From this perspective, ideas such as field, enclosure, and the definition of an intervention's limits become important. One can work by dislocation, grouping, forming new hierarchies, altering the positions of chosen materials within a specific contextual field. The relationships between advanced techniques and appropriate techniques, topology and topography, as well as the project of place and a principle of settlement become the new essentials of the architecture of modification.

Moreover, these arguments seem to converge with respect to a series of actual working circumstances.

The first is that the situation of architectural work has radically changed in Europe. The main trend of development is oriented completely toward the transformation of already urbanized areas, rather than physical expansion. One might say, as many do, that since the eighties the typical situation in Europe has involved building within the built. What exists has everywhere become our patrimony. Every architectural operation increasingly becomes an act of partial transformation within a situation: reuse, restoration, but also something new and different through the contextual relationship of already significant materials. Even urban peripheries have become places in search of an identity by means of contextual consolidation. The project as modification is also a relatively practical instrument of operation when intervening in a landscape (or what remains of this concept) through a strategy, through discrete interventions, or through minimal changes that produce vast shifts in meaning.

The second circumstance relates to the general condition of architectural thought, which has seen the decline of the great ideologies of centralized transformation and global utopias, whether for good or ill. At present, instead, it seems increasingly necessary to work on small, significant differences even when we are dealing with major scales of intervention, finding amid the site's laws of construction some materials to juxtapose with our discipline's state of advancement, as well as using those laws to pose not a grand reconstruction but rather questions and hypotheses.

Amid such questions and hypotheses, the issue of belonging undoubtedly presents a series of troubling uncertainties. First, how do we avoid the dangers of a new stylistic regionalism? Even where such regionalism defines itself as critical, how do we avoid becoming imprisoned in the character of a place, in empirical operations that reduce the project to a work of readaptation, in the dissolution of architectural form into a complete defense of the context? Project design as modification, as I have attempted to define it, must instead transform a place into an object of architecture, must reestablish the original and symbolic act of making contact with the earth, with the physical environment, with the idea of nature as the totality of all existing things, through the constitution and reconstitution of a principle of settlement.

The construction of a language of modification must therefore have solid elements at its disposal, beginning with an interpretation of the specific situation. But to find all the elements necessary for its foundation, it must also look to the goal and, beyond the goal, to the articulation of instrumental and figurative models that the discipline's tradition elaborates and transmits and that begin with other specific truths.

Every alternative that lies between model and context is of course a simplification that, as always, both clarifies and hides the truth. On the other hand, a sense of what is archetypal and what is accidental is often a question of which viewpoint is projected onto the specific situation.

An architectural monument is clearly also the invention of a new element of urban design, such as a street wall or a background for a square. The urban system finds its form through a city's unbuilt spaces, where the definition of an internal profile becomes an element of stability, connecting separately conceived parts with the complexity of the remaining urban material, which surrounds and relies on it. While the *poché* of a building plan helps us to see the stability and invention of a type, a simple shift of perception transforms this concept into a matrix for interpreting the urban context and the principle of settlement that presides over it.

Along with the idea of modification as the foundation of the project, I am also trying to describe a strategy aimed above all at minimizing errors and bypassing obstacles. Such a strategy lies far from the risky generosity practiced by the masters of modernity. Moreover, it has some troubling similarities with the uncertain notion of reform that, undefined and adaptable, permeates the politics of our time.

The idea of modification, therefore, offers no hope of definitively liberating gestures, global reconciliations, perfect consistencies, definitive utopias. The context always forms an indirect material for ensuring an architecture of place. But what the architecture of modification can offer is a description of the movement toward these unattainable values, rather than acceptance of their dissolution into contextual decoration.

A final reason supports the concept of modification. This involves a widespread longing for a reprieve from the unbearable supertechnical and superstylistic chatter of recent architectural production; a desire for sedimentation in the creative process, for a consolidation of rules in relation to specific needs, and for a return to the depth of mastery as opposed to the disoriented pandering exhibited by our current profession.

This desired reprieve will only be realized if the project becomes above all a silent modification of the specific present.

Between promises for the future and nostalgia for the integrity of the past, we must maintain the urgency of today's project. The instruments that I have sought to describe are probably the best suited to realizing this ideal.

The theme of internationalism proposed by the avant-gardes had at least two inspiring motives, on which it is useful to reflect in order to compare them with the present meaning of the word. In the first place, internationalism contributed to a polemic against nationalisms in the name of art as an absolute, nonimitative expression that took the form of geometric abstraction and analytical reason. Second, the internationalism of the avant-gardes was based on the idea of novelty and utopia as values, and on the construction, in the name of technique and progress, of a language for a classless society where the essence of a problem was the basis for its expression.

The "return to order" of the mid-twenties revolted against such ideas. This continued in the thirties with the late nationalisms of regime architectures, with the *Heimatstile,* and later with neoregionalistic tendencies, defense of local building traditions, and the theme of *mediterraneità.* Each of these positions, in turn, had its own driving motives and foundations. But although these contained many contrasts in political and ideological character, their results in the field of architecture were quite convergent.

Internationalism then reappeared in the architecture of the fifties as the reign of new procedural techniques based on concepts such as productivity, formalization of procedures in project execution, and organization of tasks, which were all thrust into the world of the project through the division of labor and specialization of production. But they also represented the value of objectivity of technique and formalization of thought as opposed to the reduction of functional rationality to mere politics and economics.

The foundations and reasons of this second neotechnical and neopositivist internationalism, which was particularly dominated by North American thought, also converged with respect to society's development in the postwar period.

The internationalism that we experience today is different. As is often stated, it represents an internationalism of nonmaterial financial currents, of scientific and technical information, and of mass communication, with their respective laws of behavior and consumption.

Some argue that this system has become so rambling, widespread, and mobile that it avoids any possibility of centralized control, and this may be good. But it also avoids any possibility of democratic control, any perspective on the common good, even any rational planning, and this is certainly very bad.

This process, whose idea of infinite possibilities excludes rules or ideologies, has created obvious difficulties regarding the foundation of any authentic difference. Subjectivity as a source of differentiation has itself weakened, with problematic consequences for forging an artistic practice of architecture.

Even the higher quality found in the interesting objects produced in the artistic field, which has its own forms of measured diversity, seems like an obstacle to the foundation of any authentic difference, since such production follows the homogenization of a market unified by mass communication, which requires continuous, indifferent inventions.

Still, we cannot effectively address this difficulty by locking ourselves within the convent of the spirit, or by pursuing a return to localisms or the fragmentation of dialects. Even less can we turn to new nationalisms, although that is the phenomenon we have right before our eyes. This is true not only for the claims for regional independence sweeping through many parts of Europe and the Soviet Union, but also for the attempt to address the great complexity of interdependencies by seeking a place of discontinuity to isolate and resolve problems while trying to define their limits and characteristics.

In the specific case of our discipline, moreover, recent years have been marked by a strong interest in context in all its various aspects: natural, historical, monumental, conservational, and reconstructional. In short, this interest has sought to open a dialogue with what exists, which is seen to possess the depth and stratification from which the site derives its specific identity, and which must be the foundation for any modification of the site.

The culture of architecture has adopted and elaborated this concern, and has substantially altered its scale of values by placing at the center of its own actions a conception of the project as a thoughtful way to maintain a critical distance while engaging the context. But we still have to conclude that the growth of cities and transformation of territories is, in the large majority of cases, headed in the opposite direction.

Indifferent to place and to historical patterns of settlement, which they constantly violate even when the rules are completely obvious, new buildings are formed and arranged according to principles derived from the forms of internationalism I described. In an ambiguous identification of progress and consumption, they model themselves on types and behaviors presented by mass communication as forms of reassurance, and signs of the advanced state of a social body.

Above all, this portrait describes the laws of formation that unite the urban peripheries of European cities. But the consolidated historical centers are also under continuous attack from such principles, which we might call principles of oriented atopia; that is, principles of settlement based on something other than the idea of place.

In urban peripheries, we often see homogeneous residential neighborhoods that lack internal hierarchies and that, because they look elsewhere, gradually lose any reference to the identity of their own existing urban centers, whose fabric and layout once served as a model for the gradual consolidation of those peripheries.

Following a severing of the ties that once linked production and service establishments to their sites through the use of local materials, energy, and labor, such peripheral establishments seem to wish to be deliberately atopical. They close themselves within their own programmatic nature, creating a scattered global system of similar functions, which are completely independent of their specific condition of settlement and which focus on repeating a behavioral as well as a functional paradigm.

To be sure, this is often a mere matter of dispersion of localization, due to banal reasons such as land costs and ease of access. However, we must realize that a decisive split has occurred between land and building. This is what has corrupted entire regions and landscapes, extreme peripheries of urban centers whose presence has now, at least in Italy, come to characterize the great roads of travel and, in general, the intersections that offer the greatest advertising opportunities.

From a tradition that once located a large factory in the countryside, near its sources of energy, or at the urban periphery, close to its sources of labor, such building-objects have either completely lost their power of spatial and social aggregation or, at their worst, completely turned these characteristics inside out.

At times, this shift involves recently formed typologies, whose immaturity regarding settlement often takes the form of a shapeless system of aggregations, with large built spaces and vast service-related terrains, which is connected to the great highway infrastructure and which remains partly hidden in those undefined spaces of conurbation that open themselves, with illogical leaps in scale, into the historical-natural landscape, squandering it completely.

We are speaking of landscapes, if we can still call them that, that are rapidly spreading. Often built according to extra-European models, they reject all integration or even any interaction with the tightly woven historical fabric of our territories.

Many years ago, toward the end of the fifties, British scholars such as Ian Nairn and Gordon Cullen attempted to offer a general interpretation of the exploding phenomenon of settlements, particularly in that undefined area between countryside and urban periphery. The phenomenon of atopia was not as evident in those years, and the fragmentation sprang more from domestic concerns. There was an attempt to understand the phenomenon in terms of its distinct novelty, by resorting to categories such as collage cities and urban surrealism. In other words, one attempted to view the phenomenon, even with all its degenerations, as part of the general process of settlement formation, observed at an incomplete phase.

But today I believe we must conclude that this is no longer the case. The phenomenon of atopia has clearly assumed an intention that places it on a totally different plane.

Supermarkets, parking lots, highway service stations, airports and their parking areas, transfer points between various means of transport, showroom centers along urban exit roads are all part of these atopical typologies. To them we must add the residual spaces, shipping container yards, used car dealerships, auto graveyards, the odd spaces between highway interchanges, unused "green spaces," junkyards, and abandoned farmlands.

Unlike the great markets of antiquity, these atopical typologies offer none of the spontaneous and temporary gathering that used to characterize those spaces *extra muros.* They are, on the contrary, regulated by relentless internal laws of distribution and equally relentless laws of investment and profit. But such laws are in no way rooted to the site. In terms of morphology and resources, they have no need for the site, because their selling point involves offering the user the momentary illusion of belonging to a different, more advanced, and more reassuring world than the one encountered in everyday life.

Atopical buildings take on the features of industrial manufacture, which uses laws of consistent performance and recognizability to guarantee the quality of the product and the safety of its handling by the user. In other words, atopical buildings have extended the rules for designing industrial products into architecture, for which they are improper.

In some ways, the social fabric that encompasses solidarity, contrasts, and a sense of belonging no longer exists for such nonplaces. Rather, a great universal void opens between the individual and the market, where the product's system of reference is completely abstract and nonspatial.

This judgment might of course result from a distortion of historical perspective on our part; one might imagine that these fragments of buildings will, in time, and against their own volition, assume a specific character and identity: specific, at least, to a historical moment and its concept of space.

Such an interpretation might be supported by the quality of settlement assumed by certain great monuments of the past that have been recontextualized with the passage of time, or that have themselves constructed new principles of settlement after the original reasons for their location had been lost. Or again, it might draw on the great systems of territorial transformation carried out by colonization, which transfers organizational models elaborated in totally extraneous sites, ranging from the Roman system of land division to the religious colonization of South America, to mention only two examples.

We could also cite the highly expressive ways that modern atopical typologies have been interpreted by the cinema (for example in a film like *Paris Texas*), or by Allen Ginsberg's prophetic poetry, or by much of contemporary painting, and thus imagine, as some argue, that we can also find authenticity in such typologies from an architectural point of view. From that perspective, it would be interesting to discuss what kinds of compatibilities are possible (and if they are possible) between the principles of identity and belonging, which architects discuss so much these days, and the principles of atopia. Whether it is possible to establish any form of interconnection between them, or how one might directly articulate the material offered by specific atopical features in terms of urban design, has at times been attempted in the past twenty years.

Perhaps the unease we feel regarding the formal organizations of these atopical typologies comes mainly because they are insufficiently radical. They do not seem able to draw significant morphological materials from their own existence outside of context, or from their own nature as celibate machines. Nor do they seem to use their extraneous state as a dialectical element with regard to their context.

Certain great products of modern engineering, for example, present (we do not know how consciously) a poetic quality based on a strong internal coherence and on a dialectic with their context.

The most obvious defect of these atopical typologies seems to be their inability to regulate the vast open spaces that functionally accompany them; or rather their inability to design such spaces so that they mediate with the surroundings and with the land (an inevitable source of support and confrontation), with its geographic and technical nature, as well as with (or consciously against) the historical depth that it encompasses.

In any case, there is no doubt that atopicality might be interpreted as a sign of an inevitable mechanism of international interdependence that is cultural as well as political and economic in structure—a sign that has yet to find a significant form of spatial organization in the territory of architecture.

Such interdependence still often takes the form of control and domination, opposing attempts by existing communities to secure the largest possible scope for their own traditions within the process of unification. Or perhaps such atopicality still facilitates the brutal exploitation of varying economic conditions among the peoples of the world.

Could it move instead toward solidarity, toward that "communicative public action" of which some philosophers speak? This is perhaps a naively positive interpretation, but one that is dictated by an intimate need and that can, at least as a hypothesis, shift the destructive impetus of atopia into architecture's own territory, transforming it into a dialogue of solidarity, even with the context.

Simplicity, as a process of adhering to the essence of use, to lack of ornament, and to mimesis of the technical reproducibility and expressive rigor of utensils, has, as we know, been the most prominent and common stylistic banner of modernity in this century.

But if one abandons the idea that a moral, tenacious pride in modesty and an egalitarian, *sachlich* striving can serve as mimeses of collective reason, progress, and liberation, then it certainly seems more difficult to enumerate the values of simplicity in times of highly complex and intense signals. At the very least, the matter of simplicity in architecture becomes subject to different possible interpretations.

Designing a simple building has become a very complicated problem, at least for those who believe that simplicity in architecture is not something natural or spontaneous, does not result from restoring linear deduction, is not tautology, simplification, a retreat from the complexity of reality, or, least of all, a relinquishing of invention.

Simplicity today stands on a dangerous ridge. One slope harbors pure opposition to market coercion, to contrivances that lack an aim or an internal reason for expression. On the other side lie in ambush oversimplification and poverty of invention, aphasia and the mannerism of poetic silence—in brief, the inarticulate superstition of simplicity.

In other words, to me simplicity is not simplification, and above all not simplification as a formal model. Eloquent simplicity can be reached through great effort, but it is never a good starting point, nor, above all, an objective at any cost. Architecture is not simple; it can only become simple.

Nor would I like, in these times of noisy, exhibitionistic redundancy of communication, to be ideologically forced to take the side of simplicity as an *a priori* mimesis of logical and moralistic rigor. That is important, but remains transitory.

The fragmentation in our times certainly calls for some solid points, some secure, well-fastened nails. But I believe that such solidity must be reconstructed not through reduction but rather by pushing project research until it succeeds in breaking through the tangled web of complication in order to rebuild, in view of the specific situation, a hypothesis for a structure that will organize architecture according to the practice of a meticulous, although consciously provisional, clarity.

It is very difficult today to imagine a return to order that could be more than a coat of whitewash over the disorder and conflicts of our times, if it does not confront the unresolvable contradictions placed daily before our eyes by notions such as logic and reason. Simplicity must make contradiction itself clear and comprehensible without denying its existence and its value as a material for establishing difference.

The reasons behind a simple building must reveal, not cover, the fissures of doubt; they must reconnect and not isolate. They must first address their own limits, and must limit the risks of instituting a law that lacks the necessary internal order. That is, they must realize that its balance is precarious, but at the same time pursue it with tenacity.

A simple building must thus compose its own image as the superficial tension of complexity; for there is no level of complexity that cannot be expressed through the clarity of simplicity without simplification.

In that sense, a building is never simple enough. To free oneself from the superfluous; that is, to identify what is superfluous without confusing it with the richness of curiosity, of a question, of questioning, requires an accurate and difficult effort toward discrimination, even though solely liberating oneself from the superfluous clearly does not guarantee access to the heart of simplicity.

A building is simple not because its shapes conform to elementary geometry, not because all of it is immediately visible, or because the logic is evident in its connections, but because all its parts voice their necessity, both reciprocally and with respect to the meaning of the specific architectural solution. In simplicity there must be nothing preestablished, nothing immobile. Instead, all must be balance, measurement, relation between points, vital organization, mysterious transparency.

It must give the impression that everything contained in the project is absolutely inevitable and certain, but that there is still always something essential beyond what has been organized.

In that sense, oscillation, cancellation, and the suspended tension of parts can also share the rigor of simplicity, and participate in the golden and absolutely general rule of economy of expression.

On the other hand, to propose simplicity in architecture is not, today, to propose a totality, a closure within a benign form of the absolute. Rather, it presents itself as the illumination of a brief fragment of truth, like the laborious deciphering of a small phrase of a text whose overall meaning remains unknown.

A simple building can also have an interior whose functions, spaces, uses, and distributions are complex; an interior rich in interrelations rather than in form, for which simplicity is, above all, a triangulation of the experimental field.

But a simple building is also the opposite of a car body that covers and unifies a complex motor constructed by a different rationality, a body that denies access to the mechanism of function and only reveals the aspect of performance. Rather, the simple building simultaneously guards and reveals its essence.

Moreover, a simple building cannot avoid referring to some attempt at refoundation, a refoundation of sense and representation that is also constructed as a reorganization of the system of functions, a radical rethinking of the reasons behind the organism and its public and contextual role.

Simple is, in that sense, also the opposite of mixed, combined. It refers to the idea of unity and homogeneity, of being devoid of possible additions, in which compositional elements endowed with autonomous life do not figure. It is, in other words, something that has reached a state in which it seems that nothing can be added or taken away, and in which all the reasons in its composition have found their own, provisionally definitive arrangement.

Architecture—great architecture—has always attempted to reduce the problems of construction, use, context, and symbolism to one single reason. The simple building carries firmly with it, even when such reasons become remote, the unitary arrangement of its components as the basis for its own specific identity.

The simplicity of a building, moreover, has to do with silence. It is the creation of a pause in the tumult of language; it identifies the divergence of sense among signs; it appears as the proud fixation of an infinite series of hesitations, tests, erasures, experiences; it is the rewriting of what we have always known. The simple project destroys all neuroses about the future, gives back to the past, to paraphrase Merleau-Ponty, not survival, which is a hypocritical form of oblivion, but a new life that takes the noble form of memory.

The simplicity of a building also represents an aspiration to find one's place near the origin of architecture itself, to look as if one had always been there, firmly fixed to the earth and to the sky, in an open discussion with the surroundings that starts with the recognition and critique of the identities and distances of each.

A simple building, in other words, rests on a principle of settlement as it does on its own physical foundations. It is the ability to clearly identify such foundations, including the connection with the earth and the geography that represents its history, that allows an architecture to achieve simplicity; that is, to become necessary in all its parts and connect itself directly to the principles of its own synthesis.

We all know that the project of architecture in our century has emphasized the importance of the process in the constitution of architectural form, or at least in one special version of it: that in which the procedure itself becomes a foundation for every significant form of project.

Thus, the constitution of architectural form is not based on a mimesis of nature, or of established models within the disciplinary tradition, or even on their interpretation. Rather, by suspending judgment on these, architecture finds its foundation in constructing a method for correlating specific problems and organizing them in meaningful ways. Above all, these become meaningful regarding the essence of the problem and its special relationship with the subject, and also regarding the discussion surrounding certain values of modernity, however widely interpreted.

Such values include techniques and productive rationales that encourage social progress, new concepts of perception and representation, and novelty itself as a value. Later, the notion of history, tradition, and memory comes into play, particularly regarding the physical context that expresses this notion, and with an emphasis on the dialectical difference between this context and every aspect of the present.

Of course, accentuating the importance of method involves not only architectural issues but also creative thought in the modern age, especially its important relationship with the rational and scientific traditions. The many significant criticisms that authoritative thinkers (and we have many today) have leveled against this tradition include accusations that it contradicts the constitution of horizons and values; that is, that the method becomes an end in itself, and thus loses a sense of its own aims.

Some critiques focus more specifically on the use of method within our discipline, and these have been repeated and applied many times in recent years.

The first of these critiques proposes that the methodological principles of modernity can easily be interpreted positivistically; that is, as pure economicism and technicism. Another suggests that modernity has not been able (due to its own nature) to ward off new formalisms and stylisms. Moreover, some have argued that modernity's demand for a new beginning at each specific question is the main obstacle to the constitution of a civil, stable language, and thus also to the possibility of a didactic transmission of architecture, an aim that is increasingly necessary in the modern situation of vast numbers of productions.

Above all (and this seems to me to be the most structural objection), it is said that no methodology is capable of producing a meaningful form (although it could produce conformation, to use the famous expression by Cesare Brandi) because the design process involves descent into a netherworld, a void packed with memory, symbols, and unexpressed needs, which cannot emerge through the methodological process but which forms the very substance of architecture.[16]

The exercise in suspension of judgment that the critical methodologies of modernity invite us to apply to the procedure of design thus gives us reasonable protection from the circularity of interpretations in the mimetic process. But this suspension can, at the same time, deprive us of essential materials for constituting the project as an expressive artistic practice. It is true that almost a century of extraordinary works of modern architecture seems to work against this idea; however, an enormous number of disasters in the built environment seem to confirm it, if one chooses to attribute to architecture those public responsibilities that the principles of modernity, which are founded on the civic duty of the project, had wanted to reclaim.

Other solutions may lie in procedures of interpretation and mimesis (we are, in some way, still talking about methods). The essence of interpretation lies in the process of contamination between languages, their metaphorical transmigration, and the weakening of specificity; this makes architecture into an event, or rather the building up of an eventuality. However, in order to practice mimesis it is necessary to refer to a model. This model could be the realm of ideas and faiths, or that of nature, or in our case it might be the concrete synthesis that a particular social group has constructed for itself in terms of architecture. This last position has been widely established for a long time, and would have the advantage (to me only an apparent advantage at present) of presenting itself as already endowed with expressive forms, thereby constituting a language of immediate communication, whose interpretation has for many centuries shown an enormous ability to adjust to problems and sites.

The field of architecture includes a finite number of traditions, founded on as many anthropological cycles as have produced such models of thought. Although some of these have definitely ended, Western culture has certainly succeeded in preserving and evolving its own model, its own classical tradition, in a particularly permanent way, despite passing through the great parenthesis of Gothic architecture. However, almost a century of buildings created by the modern movement has by now formed such a vast heritage of models and techno-morphological solutions that these can themselves be proposed as sources for interpretive mimesis. This has actually happened in recent years, mainly in stylistic terms; and at present it seems to be assuming an attitude of conciliatory preeminence that betrays its own principles. But what legitimacy can it then claim with respect to other possible mimeses?

More generally, in the absence of mimesis and contamination—that is, in the absence of significant matter transformed into memory, history, and tradition—how would it be possible to apply a method without reducing the practice of architecture to mere problem solving, to mere *operativismo*?

And finally, how can we prevent a methodological principle derived from specific conditions of the discipline's advancement from becoming an obstacle to formulating hypotheses that might lead to new and more suitable methodological rules?

As often happens in the metaphorical transactions that we architects enact, the method of which I am writing here seems very far from possessing the prerequisites of objectivity and demonstrability that are essential to the natural sciences. Instead, it seems to present continuous, indispensable digressions.

It remains true, however, that the methodological ideology constructed by modernity is also a kind of reaction to ideas that confine aesthetics to a separate and ineffable experience, parallel to the independent development of each new ideal of social organization and each scientific advancement. In other words, this prevalence of method seems to be creativity's trick for gaining access to the world by means of architecture, and for transforming it by adding the enigma of a new reality, a reality that has a special visibility, that shines by the light of its own, intimate necessity.

However, architecture cannot construct this light outside of all spatial location. It is from the very start a presence in relationships and situations, whose trace remains forever fixed in the work; and the process that forms this light has therefore a special and substantial significance.

There is also a question of establishing, through method, the rules of a practice that can meet the needs of the world, can enrich and transform our experience, but that can also fulfill architecture's responsibility to ensure a civilized nobility in what is built, and to form the recognizable environment within which collective life develops. To that end, architecture must give itself rules capable of cultivating and disseminating the profession's tradition, of dealing with the new problems and territories of the project as a discipline, and also of assuming the moral and civic responsibilities implied in the act of building.

From this perspective, the method proposed by the modern tradition is probably, despite what many critics argue, too open and free, too closely tied to wholly individual self-regulating abilities, with the possibility of developing distortions that completely contradict civil objectives. Moreover, because its program does not present models for imitation but only pathways to pursue, it fails to suit a mass market founded largely on the mimesis of behavior and appearances, and therefore on inventions that gain acceptance specifically for their transitory nature, for their constitution of metaphors built simply as metaphors, as merely aesthetic mechanisms.

We cannot deny, on the other hand, that the market and the masses, power and secularization, are the weighty narrative materials of our time, and that our refusals, our resistance, our retreats are all formed in relationship to them. Moreover, a method must be applied to these very materials, in order to organize the specific instruments required to discuss them.

With respect to all this, I believe that the use of method has the advantage of exorcising, through cold reflection, all affectations of spontaneity. It can establish a distance, a void, and thus a possibility of critical comparison, also with that which is in no way present. The method is also an exercise for the possible reconstruction of a "need to be," a professional morality that demands respect for the work's internal laws and at the same time shows the need for a continuous new beginning of the "building yard of the world."

It is not a question of siding with the autonomy of nonnarrative logic, and against expression, but of trying to offer expression a new general sense, and therefore a new architecture. We can today build only the structural outlines of such an architecture. Others, after us, will construct the facades, at a time when it becomes possible to understand the extent to which the logical, the literal, the clear eye of method, is a metaphor for the difficulties of our time.

I believe it is difficult for those of my generation to refer to the notion of image without thinking of the reflections on this subject in the famous Sartrian texts, beginning with Edmund Husserl and stretching as far as Jacques Lacan's famous essay on the self-image that the "I" constructs in the *âge du miroir*.[17] We also feel compelled to refer to all those philosophers and psychologists, as well as certain art historians (as, for example, Ernst Gombrich), who have studied the distinctions and connections between perception, image, form, and configuration.

But the relationship between image and perception that was central to those texts now forms a distant, almost always forgotten background, while everyday language, and especially the everyday language of architects, encompasses increasingly insistent talk that makes image, along with its construction and communication, into a primary objective in design, or even a measure of the quality of a project. As we shall see, this difference has important consequences, particularly for architectural design as an artistic practice.

First of all, we should note that the source of this attitude lies within the notion of the market rather than that of perception; that is, the theme of image is seized for its ability to represent and communicate, rather than for its attempts at establishing foundation.

Today, the word "image" commonly refers to that part of a thing, person, or action that appears to others, rather than to the subject that the image constructs or the method of its construction. In other words, it primarily refers to the scenario that the thing (or person or action) suggests, or to the effect produced by its appearance on the stage of the world of communication. At the roots of this phenomenon, one might naturally see the question regarding the science-driven formation of an image world as the inevitable and distinct character of modernity. It thus becomes possible to advance the hypothesis that in our century creative production no longer has direct access to reality, but only to its techno-scientific image, and that the reign of images over constitutional relationships rests on this development.

"The spectacle is capital accumulated to the point where it becomes an image," writes Guy Debord. Giorgio Agamben, commenting on this statement, tells us:

> The spectacle is nothing but the pure form of separation: when the real world is transformed into an image and images become real, the practical power of humans is separated from itself and presented as a world unto itself . . . where everything can be called into question except the spectacle itself, which, as such, says nothing but, "What appears is good, what is good appears."[18]

As we know, the relationship between image and market, or rather between image and market image, has in the past fifty years been the subject of notable critical discussion, particularly by the Frankfurt School of sociology. But some have theorized that the problem of art, and therefore of architecture, is presently restricted to restoring communication and image. By this reasoning, novelty, reality, and experience, strictly defined, no longer exist; we have only an infinite and autonomous interpretability created by the information media. Thus, image exists completely as a function of the market. It has lost its character as a basic element of the architectural object; the character, that is, of that research which (rich in fragility, in a dialoguing state of hesitation) should accompany the constitution of the architectural object during the entire process of forming meaning.

Finally, by replacing reality, the totality of market images becomes a primary source of experience and the main material for reflection and comparison in artistic practice. But this material, which is continuously remodeled by the media, is strongly homogenized in the process and thus produces a great quantity of things that are quite differently similar. On the one hand, an exploration of the media and its formidable capabilities becomes the central issue of expression, replacing any reason behind authentic image-making. On the other hand, the extension of the media web proves that not only all information but also all experience must be reproduced in order to be real.

The discipline of architecture has also suffered the assault of the notion of image as explained above.

In the first half of the sixties, there were some remarkable attempts to directly and completely adopt the market image as the central subject of architecture. The idea of urban dissolution within an isotropic communicative space, of a possible "architecture without building," also appeared at that time. "A home is not a house," Reyner Banham wrote, commenting on the famous paradigmatic image of a naked family inside a transparent bubble that was equipped with all services and perfectly autonomous, thus anticipating by many years the discourses on the immateriality of techno-scientific society.[19]

Thirty years later, the market image has assumed connotations that are more widespread and commonplace, but much less radical.

Everything has at times been resolved, at the most superficial levels, by bestowing on the information media an importance great enough to allow construction of projects loaded primarily with the weight of their role as illustration. This gives the printed and transmitted photographic image a decisive role in judgment, and shifts the much more complex and structural notion of form, with all its reasons and resistances, in the direction of decoration, atmosphere, and syllogism.

Within the process of constructing architecture, the market image has undoubtedly contributed to the problematic separation of the different aspects of technique, planning, morphology, contextual history, and project production. This process, which specializes the contribution of each, renders mute and unnecessary the relationship between varying technical and idea-driven elements, dividing the meaningful construction of architecture into separate and often inaccessible cultures. All this leads to the apparent triumph of the figurative gesturality of the "architect-creator" and his compulsion for repetition, driven above all by the need to create a marketable image.

Architects of image, who see their design task in terms of providing a few general sketches, have become conspicuously common in recent years. This has been particularly true in the United States, where such architects can rely on an advanced system of support, but we have also seen illustrious protagonists of this type in Europe.

Thus it is said that a particular architecture either has or does not have an image, implying a slippage between the real thing and that which synthetically characterizes it in terms of communication but falls far short of a complete description. If this is possible, it will condemn the object itself to a single-dimensional flattening, to living in the company of an other that improperly represents it.

The most obvious aspects of this phenomenon represent a departure from our discipline's technical heritage, or at least an impoverishment of this heritage. When dealing with great urban or territorial themes, this departure becomes a total surrender, an acceptance of their current fragmentary state. All this, in truth, perfectly corresponds to the aesthetic-sentimental reduction that the petit-bourgeois consensus contributes to these problems. We can therefore say that the architects of the market image form an organic part of the present structure of social power, but from this point of view they are also completely outside the critical tradition of modernity.

In other words, for those who work in architecture the primacy of the market image reduces focus on other project materials, toppling the sense of a reciprocal meaning of part to whole and contradicting the famous principle that every work of art should be constructed so that it contains no accessories, no form that might seem heterogeneous.

But I wonder how, in this context, we can possibly salvage for ourselves the necessary activity of compositional imagination, the thought that produces, corrects, transforms, interprets, and remembers (what Peter Handke defines as "the interiorized image" or the "image within the image"), and thus attempt to suspend, or perhaps to defer, the preoccupation with the market image and with measuring the effects of its communication.[20]

In other words, how can we preserve the time required for imagination to unfold and oscillate, to conceive that minor shift of limit and meaning that is capable, through the work, of reaching a different understanding of the world?

This does not mean that imagination should be cultivated apart from the real world, but rather that imaginative activity remains significant and transformative precisely because it is able to reconsider the hierarchies and nature of the world's materials from their inception; that is, to discuss the reasons that have formed the market image.

Moreover, by the nature of its long, complex efforts, carried out through many confrontations, changes, and diverse contributions, as well as through the dialogues of multiple subjects, architecture has a vital need to extend the act of image construction throughout the entire process of design. I am convinced that, to varying degrees, this forms a specific element of every artistic practice.

For us, Aristotle's famous phrase "Art is the ability to create truth by reflection" (if it refers, albeit improperly, to imagination as an activity, rather than as the mere recollection of images) can be interpreted in the sense that imagination and reflection, in their continuous interchange, can still construct new pieces of reality, thus modifying and enriching the world of our experiences.[21]

Notes

Notes to the Foreword by Kenneth Frampton

1. Vittorio Gregotti, "Clues," *Casabella*, no. 484 (October 1982), 13.
2. Vittorio Gregotti, "In Praise of Technique," *Casabella*, no. 480 (May 1982), 15.
3. *Inside Architecture*, 5.
4. *Inside Architecture*, 11.
5. *Inside Architecture*, 40.
6. *Inside Architecture*, 65.
7. See Donald A. Schön, *The Reflective Practitioner: How Professionals Think in Action* (New York: Basic Books, 1983).

Notes to the Translator's Introduction

1. *Inside Architecture*, 22.
2. Jürgen Habermas, "Modernity—An Incomplete Project," in Hal Foster, ed., *The Anti-Aesthetic: Essays On Postmodern Culture* (Port Townsend, Washington: Bay Press, 1983), 3–15.
3. *Inside Architecture*, 25.
4. Walter Benjamin, "The Task of the Translator," in *Illuminations*, ed. Hannah Arendt, trans. Harry Zohn (New York: Schocken Books, 1969), 69–82.

Notes to *Inside Architecture*

Translators' note: The original Italian version of *Inside Architecture* did not include bibliographic references or endnotes. We have therefore, with advice from the author, researched and listed this information for further use by the reader. Where possible, English translations of foreign texts have been cited.

1. See Paolo Rossi, "Scienza della natura e scienze umane: la dimenticanza e la memoria," *Casabella*, no. 577 (March 1991), 39.

2. Paul K. Feyerabend, *Dialogo sul metodo* (Bari: Laterza, 1989), 71.

3. This lecture, given by Theodor Adorno in Berlin to the German Werkbund on October 23, 1965, was originally published in German as "Functionalismus heute," *Die Neue Rundschau*, 77, no. 4 (1966). An English version entitled "Functionalism Today," translated by Jane Newman and John Smith, was published in *Oppositions*, no. 17 (Summer 1979), 31–41.

4. Elias Canetti, *Crowds and Power*, trans. Carol Stewart (New York: Viking Press, 1962).

5. Joseph Rykwert, *On Adam's House in Paradise: The Idea of the Primitive Hut in Architectural History* (Cambridge: MIT Press, 1981).

6. Husserl's version reads, "We must also inquire back into the original meaning of the handed-down geometry, which continued to be valid with this very same meaning—continued and at the same time was developed further, remaining simply 'geometry' in all its new forms." Edmund Husserl, "The Origin of Geometry," in *The Crisis of European Sciences and Transcendental Philosophy*, trans. David Carr (Evanston: Northwestern University Press, 1970), 353.

7. Gianni Vattimo, *The Transparent Society*, trans. David Webb (Baltimore: Johns Hopkins University Press, 1992), 72. *Wesen*, a term used by Heidegger, refers to the fundamental hypersensitive and excitable experience associated with the art and aesthetics of late modernity. For Heidegger, this experience is perceptually as well as morally oscillating, disorienting, and shocking for modern man.

8. See Massimo Cacciari, "Nihilismo e progetto," *Casabella*, no. 483 (September 1982), 50–51; and "Progetto," *Laboratorio Politico*, 2/1982.

9. See Vittorio Gregotti, "Conservazioni," *Casabella*, no. 565 (February 1990), 2.

10. Aldo Gargani, "Sogni esauditi," *Leggere*, no. 40 (1992), 42.

11. Alexandre Koyré, "Du monde de l'à peu près à l'univers de la précision," *Critique*, no. 28 (September 1948), 807–808.

12. Max Bense, *Razionalismo e sensibilità* (Milan: Bompiani, 1963), 76. Published in German as *Rationalismus und Sensibilität Präsentationen* (Krefeld: Agis-Verlag, 1956).

13. See Ernesto N. Rogers, *Auguste Perret* (Milan: Il Balcone, 1955), 49.

14. Gropius's response to a symposium entitled "In Search of a New Monumentality," published in *The Architectural Review*, 104, no. 624 (September 1948), 127.

15. "History is that which transforms documents into monuments." Michel Foucault, *The Archaeology of Knowledge*, trans. A. M. Sheridan Smith (New York: Pantheon Books, 1972), 7.

16. Cesare Brandi, *Struttura ed architettura* (Turin: Einaudi, 1967), 39.

17. See Jacques Lacan, *Ecrits*, trans. Alan Sheridan (New York: Norton, 1977), 1–7. Also refer to Lacan's "The Looking-Glass Phase," *International Journal of Psychoanalysis*, 1937.

18. Guy Debord, *Society of the Spectacle*, trans. Donald Nicholson-Smith (New York: Zone Books, 1994), 24. Giorgio Agamben, *The Coming Community*, trans. Michael Hardt (Minneapolis: University of Minnesota Press, 1993), 79–80.

19. Reyner Banham, "A Home Is Not a House," *Art in America*, no. 2 (April 1965), 70–79. The article was republished, with original illustrations by François Dallegret, in Banham's *Design by Choice*, ed. Penny Sparke (New York: Rizzoli, 1981), 56–60.

20. Peter Handke, *Intervista sulla scrittura* (Bergamo: Lubrina Editore, 1990), 17. Published in German as *Aber ich lebe nur von den Zwischenräument* (Frankfurt: Suhrkamp, 1987).

21. This point arises in Aristotle's discussion of imitation, where he writes, "Though the objects themselves may be painful to see, we delight to view the most realistic representations of them in art." Aristotle, *De poetica*, chap. 4, 1448b, in *The Works of Aristotle*, trans. Ingram Bywater (Oxford: Clarendon Press, 1928).

A Letter from Tony Dungy

As a professional football coach, I spend a lot of time meeting with our team's players to help them improve. The number one teaching aid we coaches have for them is our playbook. It includes all the information they'll need to do their jobs and be successful on the field. We refer to the playbook in our meetings and also encourage them to take it home to study because the book is filled with information to make playing the game much easier. As coaches, we want our players to know the playbook inside and out *before* they go out on the field.

The Bible is God's playbook for us. It has the information we need to enjoy life and to do his will. We would benefit from reading God's playbook before we hit the field, too, but we don't always do that. Often we go to the Bible only after we've gotten into a tough situation. This is like a player trying to read his playbook once we've gotten behind or after the game is over. It may help, but not as much as knowing what to do beforehand, so he can make the right decisions during the game.

Often when we have a player who isn't playing up to his potential, it's because he's not sure exactly what to do on the field. We always encourage those players to "get in their book." While they are studying, the coaches are always there to answer questions they might have.

You may not be enjoying life as much as you could or be living up to your potential for the Lord. Getting into his book, the Bible, is the best way to improve your life. And like a good head coach, God is always there—through prayer—to answer questions about those things in his Word that we might not understand. I encourage you to read the Bible and to pray, communicating with God daily. That's the best way to be successful in the game of life.